KAUFMAN AT THE MOVIES

Articles & Essays 1987–2021
Volume 2

J.B. KAUFMAN

GREENVIEW
PRESS

© 2022 J.B. Kaufman
All rights reserved.

Published by Greenview Press, LLC. No part of this book may be reproduced or transmitted in any form or by any means, electronic or mechanical, including photocopying, recording, or by any information storage and retrieval system, without written permission from the publisher.

Design: Steven Reeser
Project management: Virginia Reeser
Special thanks to Barrett Morgan, Jim Hollifield, and Mike Vaughn
Back cover photo: Valerio Greco

www.jbkaufman.com

Library of Congress Cataloging-in-Publication Data on file.

ISBN 978-0-578-36917-4

Printed in the United States of America

Contents

1   Introduction

4   *The Unpardonable Sin*, An Unmarketable Film
[first published 1989]

16   Fascinating Youth: The Story of the Paramount Pictures School
[first published 1990]

48   *Public Opinion* and the Waite Murder Case
[first published 1996]

56   "It Was Always Funny Working With Fields": Producing *Sally of the Sawdust* and *That Royle Girl*
[first published 1998]

92   A Lost and Found *Romance*
[first published 2013]

104   Footloose Widows in Havana: The Changing Face of Warner Bros. Comedy, 1926–1933
[not previously published]

131   Volume 2 Bibliography

134   Index

Introduction
to both volumes

I first discovered the movies at age five. The occasion was a reissue of Walt Disney's *Cinderella*, and my parents had taken my brother and me to a local theater to see it. The memory is still vivid in my mind. Here were artists' drawings—*beautiful* drawings that *moved*—and, moreover, moved on a surface as big as the side of a building. I was overwhelmed with wonder, and at this point I can say that it was literally a life-changing experience. From that time on I was obsessed. Partly, of course, with animation, that miracle of drawings that seemed to come to life; and indeed animation has remained close to my heart in all the years since then. But my obsession soon grew beyond animation to embrace the larger world of movies in general. That fateful visit to a movie theater was soon followed by others, where I savored both Walt Disney's animated classics and his more recent live-action films. Before long I was hopelessly preoccupied with the magical world I had discovered inside a movie theater. At first I merely wanted a theater of my own, so I could enjoy that enchanting experience every day. As time passed and my awareness deepened, I raised my sights: now I wanted to *be* Walt Disney, and produce wonderful movies like that myself. (Single-handed, of course.)

My discovery of film *history* didn't occur until a few years later, when I was twelve. Until then, I suppose I thought of movies as existing in a kind of eternal Now. That all changed on a visit to an aunt and uncle whose house was filled with books. Spotting a volume titled *Agee on Film*, I snatched it up—although, at that time, I had never heard of James Agee—and plunged into the first chapter: a reprint of Agee's landmark 1949 essay, "Comedy's Greatest Era." It was another pivotal moment in my life. Like most people I knew, I had never given silent movies a second thought, but Agee's eloquent tribute to the great silent comedians opened my eyes. Initially I was drawn to the brilliance of Chaplin, Keaton, and the other comedians Agee had celebrated, and inevitably this led me to discover the entire glorious world of silent cinema. Now my focus shifted, and my original obsession with movies matured into a passion for *classic* movies, Disney and otherwise.

Life has followed its circuitous, unpredictable path in the decades since then, and along the way I've discovered additional interests, some of which are still with me. But that core fascination with classic film remained and, if anything, grew stronger. Eventually I found myself in a position to conduct my own research into that enthralling world, to learn for myself how some of my favorite classics had been produced, and even to conduct interviews with some of the people who had made them. Now my lifelong passion blossomed into a career, as I was given the opportunity to publish articles and books on film history.

I'm amazed to realize, as I write this, that I've been turning out short-form pieces—articles, essays, festival program notes, and so on—intermittently for more than thirty years. Most of them have long since disappeared from print. In this volume and its companion, I've rounded up some of the better pieces for reprinting, along with a couple of new ones. Collectively they represent a cross-section of the vast range of movies that have captivated me since childhood: silent films, sound films, features and short subjects, both animated and live-action. The reader will notice that all of these pieces are about American productions; not that I haven't learned to love the classic films of other countries, but only that I still don't know enough about them to do them justice in print. For that matter, the world of *American* classics is still so endless and unexplored that my journey of discovery is still very much in progress. The articles in these pages reflect only the progress I've made to date.

It's a blessing to be able to revisit these essays—after a long absence, in some cases—partly because it gives me a second chance to get them right! Thirty years of practice do help a writer to sharpen his skills, and for this anthology I've had a welcome opportunity to edit the earlier pieces and repair some awkwardly written passages. In addition, I may as well admit that time has brought to light some embarrassing factual mistakes in some of the earlier articles, and I haven't hesitated to correct those mistakes for this edition. For this I beg the reader's indulgence; it seems more important to me to introduce *accurate* information into the literature than to wallow in public penance for my younger self's mistakes. In the interest of transparency I've owned up to the more substantial changes in the individual introductions, but the texts themselves have been silently corrected wherever it seemed necessary. In a couple of cases they've also been expanded far beyond their original length, where new information has come to light in the meantime, or where the original publication simply didn't permit adequate space.

With all of that in mind . . . welcome to my world! Special thanks to my late beloved parents, for all those trips to the movies (among so many other things); to Mr. Disney and Mr. Agee for those primal early experiences; to my wife Margaret, who has patiently supported these endeavors and contributed materially to some of them; to an army of friends and colleagues, some of them named in these pages, who have helped so much in pulling together all this information and getting it published in the first place; specifically, at the moment, to my dear friends Steve and Virginia Reeser, and Barrett Morgan, all of whom have played essential roles in bringing this anthology to fruition; and above all to God, for granting me a life in which I have the luxury of pursuing this passion. And thanks too to you, the reader, for sharing these adventures with me. I hope they will bring you some measure of the joy they have brought, and continue to bring, to me.

J.B. Kaufman
April 2021

The Unpardonable Sin, an Unmarketable Film

First published: *Griffithiana* 35/36 (Ottobre 1989), pp. 151–59 (including separate Italian translation). Reprinted by permission.

I first met silent-film legend Blanche Sweet in 1984, and during the next two years, until her death in 1986, conducted a series of interviews with her about her extraordinary career. By the time of her death I had determined to write a book about her, and promptly plunged into the archival research for the project—a project which, despite numerous interruptions, is still in progress at this writing. In the meantime, thanks to the kind help of Russell Merritt, I came to know the wonderful folks at La Cineteca del Friuli in Italy, who annually stage the great silent-film festival in Pordenone. Encouraged to write an article for their journal Griffithiana, *I responded with this piece about one of Blanche's most unusual films. As far as I know,* The Unpardonable Sin *is still a lost film, but the story behind it is still as remarkable as ever. I've learned more about it since this article was first published and have updated the text accordingly, and have also rewritten some passages that really needed rewriting.*

Thank you: Blanche Sweet, Kevin Brownlow, Steven and Mary Higgins, Russell Merritt, Piera Patat and Livio Jacob, and David Mayer and Helen Day-Mayer.

THE UNPARDONABLE SIN

AN UNMARKETABLE FILM

In his essential book *The War, the West, and the Wilderness*, Kevin Brownlow has written of the producers of silent films about World War I, whose films were still unfinished at the time of the Armistice. They had expected to capitalize on wartime passions, only to find that those passions—and much of their potential audience—disappeared virtually overnight when the war was over.[1] A prime example of this phenomenon was *The Unpardonable Sin* (1918, released 1919), starring Blanche Sweet and directed by Marshall Neilan. This film told an inflammatory tale of the German army's brutality against helpless victims, and it was *almost* finished when the war ended. Sure enough, its war-oriented story suddenly became a handicap, as the peacetime audience sought relief from anything related to the war. Yet the film eventually overcame this obstacle and even achieved a substantial success, thanks to a creative (but less than honest) publicity campaign by its producer.

That producer was a colorful ex-baseball player named Harry Garson, who had scored a coup by luring Blanche Sweet back to the screen after an absence of more than a year. Other producers had been clamoring for her services, but Garson, whose independence appealed to

Blanche's own independent spirit, succeeded where they had failed. Under his management, in mid-1918, she appeared in *The Hushed Hour*, supported by a cast that included Rosemary Theby, Wilfred Lucas, and Kid McCoy (Norman Selby). The film was finished by late June, and Garson took it east to New York to make distribution arrangements. He was also looking for a story property for his next production. Even before arriving in New York, he had hit on the idea of filming a sensational new book called *The Unpardonable Sin*, written by Rupert Hughes.

Hughes, one of the most popular writers of the 1910s, was no stranger to movie audiences; numerous films had already been based on his novels. In addition, he had a fairly strong military orientation. He had been a member of the National Guard of New York from 1897 to 1908, advancing in rank from private to first lieutenant, and had been reappointed to a captaincy early in 1916. Asked by an interviewer in May 1917 what authors could do to help in the war effort, Hughes wasted no words: they should enlist! He also had this to say about the effect of war on literature:

> War destroys generalizations. War brings things down to cases and gives writers a sense of actuality . . . The process is interesting. A mother gives up her son—this act is observed and celebrated by the popular songwriter. The resulting "mother-song" is trite and banal, and only buffoons sing it. Then suddenly it comes to us that what the song says really is important—that the tears of mothers and the cries of the wounded are tremendous things, the stuff of literature. The things that the "mother-song" says ought not to be tiresome, the trouble is with the way in which they are said in the song. We see that the writer's task is to find a new way of saying these things. We see that writers have been afraid to be heroic, but that now they must be heroic, must write of the great elemental and immortal passions.[2]

Taking his own advice, Hughes produced *The Unpardonable Sin*— a novel that may have seemed, at the time, simply an account of the great elemental passions, but today seems virulent propaganda. First published serially in *Red Book* magazine, then in hard covers by Harper & Brothers in June 1918, the book was an immediate success. Its story concerned the Parcot family: father, mother, and daughters Dimny and Alice. The father, a famous explorer, was conveniently dispatched on an arctic expedition before the story even began, so that he was not on hand to protect his wife and daughters. At the outbreak of war in Belgium in 1914, the mother took it upon herself to travel to that beleaguered country, remove Alice from the Belgian convent school she was attending, and bring her home to California. But she was too late, and both mother and daughter, along with the innocent Belgian civilians, fell prey to the invading German army—the "unpardonable sin" in this case including the rapes of both mother and daughter. Shortly thereafter Dimny, still in California, received a letter from Alice apprising her of their fate, and suggesting that their shame was so great that it would be better to think of them as dead. Of course Dimny disregarded this request, and the rest of the story detailed her adventures in reaching Belgium in an attempt to rescue them—a feat which was not accomplished without the aid of an heroic male companion.

Published after America's entry into the war, *The Unpardonable Sin* did not risk violating any concept of neutrality. The book, and its instant success, were firmly tied to the pro-war, anti-German fervor of the times. At one point the reader was told that the hero, who was of partly German extraction, felt that he must do something "that might atone somewhat for the German blood in his veins. He had come to regard it as a vicious principle in his system, an inherited disease." The reader was clearly expected to approve of this viewpoint. In fact, this passage was quoted by the *New York Times* book reviewer, who went on to comment that "the immensity of the tragedy involved [had] apparently had a subduing effect upon Mr. Hughes's usually rather flamboyant style"![3]

For further evidence of the volatile atmosphere in which this project took shape, we need look no further than Blanche Sweet herself. Anyone who knew Blanche, at any time in her life, can testify that she was a strong, independent thinker, never given to following the crowd.

In 1915 she was genuinely neutral in her feelings about the European war. A writer who interviewed her for *Photoplay* reported: "She likes to read about the war, but is still undecided as to her preference for the ultimate victor. She is especially interested in submarines and talks like a naval expert about the new German submarines which have a steaming radius of 2,500 miles."[4] But the wave of hatred that accompanied America's entry into the war was so pervasive that Blanche was swept along with it. In the spring of 1918, the same publication quoted her as saying: "The war must be fought to prevent Germany becoming the ruler of the world. It would be unthinkable. Germany is too cruel and exacting. When I say cruel I do not mean the physical cruelty of the Germans toward the Belgians.[5] I mean something deeper and more essential than that. After all, the world can endure a good deal of physical cruelty. The reason why a Teutonic world could not be endured is this: Germany expects all the weak and inefficient nations of the world to behave like officers on the General Staff in Berlin. She expects an efficiency that less intense races are incapable of. When you come to analyze this, it becomes evident that there could be no sharper cruelty. Germany must never be a world ruler. She expects too much perfection."[6]

In this highly charged wartime climate, it seemed that Harry Garson could hardly have found a better commercial proposition for his next production than *The Unpardonable Sin*. Blanche was agreeable, and it was determined that she would appear in a dual role (something she had already done in several earlier films) as both sisters. Marshall Neilan, who had directed some of Blanche's earlier films and who was to marry her a few years later, was signed as director. In addition to Blanche, the cast included Wallace Beery—who was frequently cast as villains at this stage in his career—as the vile Col. Klemm, who committed the worst of the atrocities against the Parcot women.[7] Freckle-faced young Wesley Barry, who had appeared in some of Mary Pickford's films and who would work again with Neilan in later years, was cast in a comic-relief role as "George Washington Sticker," an irrepressible little American refugee. In the general excitement over filming this popular novel, *The Hushed Hour* was temporarily forgotten.

The company entrained for the West Coast to begin work immediately on *The Unpardonable Sin*, and its release was tentatively announced for 15 October 1918. If this date had been met, Garson might have been spared some serious problems later on.

But delays, never uncommon in filmmaking, conspired to slow production. The most serious delay was caused by the Spanish influenza epidemic, which—in addition to its disastrous toll in human lives—had resulted in a partial ban on Hollywood production. Garson's company was allowed to continue working, but was required to distribute flu masks to all non-acting personnel. The players, too, were expected to wear the masks between takes. Blanche later told DeWitt Bodeen: "When the cameras weren't turning, everybody had to don a flu mask. I was in nearly every shot, playing one sister or the other and I finally said 'to hell with it' and wouldn't wear a mask at all."[8] No one is known to have contracted the flu during the making of *The Unpardonable Sin*, but the delays turned out to be more significant than anyone realized at the time.

At this point in the story one of Harry Garson's most characteristic talents begins to emerge: a gift for hyperbole and a casual disregard for the truth. Knowing that he had a potentially hot property on his hands, he capitalized on the opportunity to issue production anecdotes to the trade press and to embellish them whenever possible. The flu-mask story, as reported by Blanche, was interesting enough. But when Garson told the same story to the press, he included some veiled allusions to string-pulling with local government officials; and it was revealed that the shooting of one

Wallace Beery, as a loathsome German officer, confronts Blanche Sweet in *The Unpardonable Sin*.

big scene required the presence on the set of one policeman from every district in Los Angeles, along with ten doctors and twenty-five nurses![9]

As production dragged along, the release date for the film was pushed back to the first of November, then the first of December. But negotiations between the U.S. and Germany, hinging on Woodrow Wilson's Fourteen Points, were already under way, and the writing was on the wall. Wilson (who had always opposed the German-atrocity films anyway) was concerned that American filmmakers were still not getting the message, and he asked the Committee on Public Information, the "Creel Committee," to contact them with a polite but firm request. If war pictures were still to be made, the inflammatory scenes of German brutality must be soft-pedaled or, better still, eliminated altogether.[10]

However this request may have been received by other filmmakers, it struck the *Unpardonable Sin* company like a thunderbolt. "From the government came the warning: 'No more atrocities'," Blanche recalled, "and we knew the war was over. And it was. The newspapers found out

The *Unpardonable Sin* camera crew, masked for protection from the flu. This photo, originally published in *Photo-Play Journal* (January 1919), acquired a dark new topicality during the COVID-19 pandemic of 2020, and was adopted by Le Giornate del Cinema Muto as the thematic image of its (virtual) festival that year. Courtesy Media History Digital Library.

about it two days later."[11] The film was nearly finished by this time, but the company was forced to face an unpleasant truth: they had completed their picture just as the potential market for it began to crumble.

In the ensuing struggle to sell the film, Garson's mendacity was sorely tested. A chronological reading of trade-press coverage over the next four months is both funny and sad. The Los Angeles premiere date was announced, then moved back; then a different theater was selected for the event. Then it was announced that the film would open, not in Los Angeles, but in New York—but the date and location continued to fluctuate. Then the event was announced for Los Angeles after all. And all the while Garson continued to issue success stories to the press: he had so many offers that it was impossible to choose between them. At one point he claimed to have rejected a $200,000 offer for the outright sale of the negative.[12]

Ever mindful of the commercial value of controversy, Garson was careful to stress this element as well. Early in September a disgruntled reader, unable to find a copy of Hughes' novel at a New York library, had written an anonymous letter to the *New York Times* in which he charged "censorship at its very worst."[13] E.H. Anderson, director of the New York public libraries, had hastened to answer the charge in the next day's edition of the *Times*, declaring that the libraries under his jurisdiction had purchased as many copies of the book as they could afford. Now Garson seized on the incident and tried to inflate those two letters to the status of a major national controversy.[14]

At one point a member of the trade press did manage to pin Garson down to the fact that he was trying to sell a war film to a postwar audience. Garson's response: the film was "particularly timely"! "When I say that this production is particularly timely," he went on, "I must be given credit for reading the newspapers and therefore know that the War is ended and that the influenza also has practically finished its course. The people are now in the mood for good, clean, substantial entertainment. But a motion picture production must have exceptional merit if it expects to keep in the so-called 'special' class. Many scenes of *The Unpardonable Sin* depict Belgium. During the many years to be spent in the period of re-construction of that country it will always be a keenly interesting and absorbing topic."[15] But all of Garson's bluffing could not hide the increasingly obvious act that he was attempting to peddle a product that no one wanted. And to an independent producer, without a guaranteed network of distribution, this was a matter of crucial importance.

Garson finally solved his dilemma by taking matters into his own hands. Completed in mid-November 1918, *The Unpardonable Sin* was given its world premiere on 2 March 1919—not in Los Angeles, not in New York, not in Chicago, but in Detroit. Why Detroit? Because Garson owned a theater there. He had begun his association with the film business, years earlier, by acquiring the Broadway Strand theater in Detroit. Now, if no one else would open his film, he would open it himself. By this time Blanche Sweet and Marshall Neilan had, understandably, grown distrustful of Garson. Learning that he was to premiere *The Unpardonable Sin* in his own theater, they feared that he might have tampered with the film after its nominal completion. Blanche, who was taking a trip east anyway, arranged to attend the Detroit opening incognito. "Marshall, like many directors of today," she explained, "wanted to do it his way, and that no one would interfere with it. Well, he got the idea that Harry Garson was going to play some tricks, take some scenes out or put some scenes in, change the script . . . We had a definite suspicion that that's what he was going to do. Because that was why I went to Detroit, to look at *The Unpardonable Sin*. But from the look of it, it seemed that he really hadn't done much to it at all."[16]

The troubled history of this film has rarely been touched upon in print. When it has been documented at all, writers have sometimes assumed, because of the initial difficulties, that the picture was a financial failure. In fact, however, this was not the case. A story as convoluted as this deserves one more ironic twist, and *The Unpardonable Sin* delivered one. That initial Detroit showing opened to a wildly successful reception, and as hundreds of patrons continued to line up at the Broadway Strand box office day after day, the national trade press began to take notice. Ultimately the Detroit engagement lasted for a solid month, and exhibitors from the major markets, suddenly galvanized, rushed to book the film for their own territories. Garson had defied the usual conventions of exhibition, and now his gamble was paying off handsomely. PICTURE HISTORY MADE IN DETROIT, announced a headline in *Moving Picture World*,[17] and as the spring of 1919 stretched into summer and autumn, each week brought new success stories.

Reversing the usual procedure, the New York opening took place exactly two months after the premiere in Detroit. ("So much has been written about *The Unpardonable Sin* from its out of town presentations," grumbled the *Variety* reviewer, "that a review of the picture at this time seems somewhat belated."[18]) Everywhere the film was shown, it met with enthusiastic audiences and healthy box-office receipts. *Variety* went on to term the film "a certain sensational box office attraction everywhere,"[19] and the Palace Theatre in Superior, Wisconsin reported receipts within $200 of the record established by *The Birth of a Nation*.[20] Critics, too, endorsed the film. Despite some mild carping at the fresh airing of German atrocities after the war's end, most reviewers enthusiastically recommended the film itself. "The whole picture looms as a real epic of drama," said one.[21]

But the surprising success of *The Unpardonable Sin* came too late to mend the strained relationship between Blanche and Neilan, on one hand, and Harry Garson on the other. *The Hushed Hour* was dusted off and released in mid-1919, to a lukewarm reception. (Once again the premiere was held at Garson's Broadway Strand theater in Detroit, perhaps in an attempt to repeat his earlier success.) After that Blanche's business arrangement with Garson was quietly terminated, and she signed with Jesse D. Hampton instead. Working with Garson had been a memorable experience, but it was one that Blanche Sweet, for one, was not anxious to repeat.

By 1919, the publication of title songs had become a popular promotional tool to help publicize new movies. *The Unpardonable Sin* was no exception. According to Arthur Lamb's lyric, the "unpardonable sin" was a man's careless disregard of a woman's true love. Courtesy David Mayer and Helen Day-Mayer.

Notes

1. Brownlow, *The War, the West, and the Wilderness*, pp. 171–72.
2. Rupert Hughes quoted in *New York Times*, 13 May 1917, VI:13:1–2.
3. *The Unpardonable Sin* book review, *New York Times*, 30 June 1918, V:298:1–2.
4. K. Owen, "The Girl on the Cover," *Photoplay*, April 1915, p. 92.
5. This statement might at first appear to be a shrewd bit of promotion for *The Unpardonable Sin*—except that it was made before the book had even been published!
6. Blanche Sweet quoted by Harry Carr in "Waiting for Tomorrow," *Photoplay*, May 1918, p. 117.
7. Beery played a similarly despicable German officer in Irvin Willat's *Behind the Door*, also released in 1919.
8. Blanche Sweet quoted by DeWitt Bodeen in "Blanche Sweet," p. 557.
9. See "Sweet Picture Comes Through," *Motion Picture News*, 30 November 1918, p. 3239.
10. See Brownlow, *The War, the West, and the Wilderness*, p. 158; and Campbell, *Reel America and World War I*, pp. 110–11.
11. Blanche Sweet to author, 1 July 1984.
12. See "Harry Garson Says He Has Turned Down $200,000 for Blanche Sweet Film, 'The Unpardonable Sin'," *Exhibitors Trade Review*, 28 December 1918.
13. Letters, *New York Times*, 3 September 1918, 10:5.
14. See "Garson Special Ready in Nov.", *Motion Picture News*, 26 October 1918, p. 2668.
15. "Blanche Sweet's Latest Called Timely," *Motion Picture News*, 23 November 1918, p. 3081.
16. Blanche Sweet to author, 4 July 1985.
17. *Moving Picture World*, 15 March 1919, p. 1459.
18. *The Unpardonable Sin* review, *Variety* ("Jolo"), 9 May 1919, p. 52.
19. Ibid.
20. See "Friedman Scores with 'Unpardonable Sin'," *Motion Picture News*, 20 September 1919, p. 2436.
21. *The Unpardonable Sin* review, *Motion Picture News* (Peter Milne), 17 May 1919, p. 3270.

The Unpardonable Sin

Blanche Sweet Feature Corporation/Harry Garson, 2 March 1919
Not copyrighted
8 reels

Director: Marshall Neilan
Scenario: George Richelavie, based on the novel by Rupert Hughes
Camera: Tony Gaudio
CAST: Blanche Sweet (Alice Parcot/Dimny Parcot)
Edwin Stevens (Stephen Parcot)
Mary Alden (Mrs. Parcot)
Matt Moore (Noll Winsor)
Wesley Barry (George Washington Sticker)
Wallace Beery (Col. Klemm)
Bull Montana (The Brute)
Bobby Connolly (Boy Scout)

North American opening dates, 1919
Detroit: 2 March, Broadway Strand Theater
Toronto: 31 March, Allen Theater
San Francisco: 6 April, California Theater
Los Angeles: 13 April, Kinema Theater
Chicago: 20 April, Randolph Theater
New York: 2 May, Broadway Theater
Minneapolis: 4 May, New Lyric Theater
St. Paul: 11 May, New Liberty Theater
Newark: 26 May, Broad Street Theater
Atlanta: 3 June, Criterion Theater

Fascinating Youth: The Story of the Paramount Pictures School

First published: *Film History*, 1990 (vol. 4 no. 2), pp. 131–151. Reprinted by permission.

Of all the major studios in Hollywood history, one of my favorites is Paramount Pictures. The sheer variety and scope of production during Paramount's heyday is endlessly captivating. While reading up on some of the studio's major silents of the 1920s, I kept running across references to the Paramount Pictures School of 1925–26, and was intrigued. The more I learned about it, the more fascinating it became. Through a series of circumstances I had the great good fortune to interview two graduates of the school—and, since another of the students had been a native of my own home town, I had a highly unusual advantage in accessing primary research materials. Moreover, Richard Koszarski, then the editor of Film History, *was able to provide still more primary documents since his offices were located at the former Paramount studio in Astoria, where the school had been located. The result was this article. Here again I've made an effort to polish the writing, but the substance of the article is largely the same as when first published.*

Thank you: Charles "Buddy" Rogers, Greg Blackton, Kevin Brownlow, Richard Koszarski, Pat Blue (and her brothers, Tom and Mike Lynch), Beverly Henline; Sam Gill and Howard Prouty (Margaret Herrick Library, Academy of Motion Picture Arts and Sciences); Ned Comstock and Anne Schlosser (Cinema-TV Library, University of Southern California); Microtext Division, Boston Public Library; and John Cavallo, Miles Kreuger, Russell Merritt, Barry Paris, George Turner, and Ben Urish.

FASCINATING YOUTH

THE STORY OF
THE PARAMOUNT PICTURES SCHOOL

Tucked away among the other widely varying titles in Paramount Pictures' release schedule for 1925–1926 was a true oddity: a seven-reel feature called *Fascinating Youth*, which was, indeed, fascinating. It was not only a commercial Paramount release, but also a screen test of sorts—for, not one, but *sixteen* potential contractees. It also amounted to a graduation exercise, for the sixteen players in question were the graduates of an acting school established by the studio, the Paramount Pictures School. This was a bold, innovative experiment on Paramount's part, an attempt to develop a home-grown stock company out of unknown and largely inexperienced young talent. It produced at least two stars who would contribute materially to the films of the late silent and early sound period. And it was an experiment that was never to be repeated.

The idea of a training program for Paramount players was not a new one; various ideas had been circulating within the company for several years. In 1922 the studio had announced the Paramount Stock Company School, complete with administrative officers, a faculty (all selected from the Paramount payroll, of course), and rules of conduct. But this was, as its name implies, a training course for players who were already established with the company. Other experiments in later years would likewise draw on the studio's existing talent roster.

In the spring of 1925, Jesse L. Lasky, vice-president of Famous Players-Lasky, publicly announced his concern over a problem facing motion-picture executives. The industry had, as the *New York Times* paraphrased it, "not been able to recruit a sufficient number of actors and actresses to meet the ever-increasing requirements."[1] To combat this problem, Lasky proposed the formation of a national acting school, to be located at the company's East Coast studio at Astoria, Long Island. "Up to the present time," Lasky explained, "the acquisition of playing material has been left more or less to chance; any search for artists has been haphazard and, for the most part, ineffectual. The establishment of the Paramount Picture [sic] School, Inc., is the first step toward putting on a practical basis the motion-picture industry's effort to augment its number of artists . . . It is our hope that by means of this school the young men and women of real talent may win their opportunity in pictures without the heartaches, the privations and the defeats which face the beginner under the present conditions."[2]

The formation of the school, officially incorporated on 18 March 1925, was announced nationally in newspapers and fan magazines. "What West Point or Annapolis does for the patriotic young man," *Photoplay* noted, "this school will do for the ambitious screen aspirant of either sex."[3] The school boasted a distinguished board of directors: Lasky, Adolph Zukor, Joseph Hergesheimer, Daniel Frohman, Gilbert Miller, John Emerson, Thomas Meighan, and D.W. Griffith. Most of these people actually had little or nothing to do with the operation of the school. Griffith, who had just begun working for Paramount, was tacked on to the list simply because of the prestige associated with his name. Recruitment of applicants for the first term was announced for a period running from early April to mid-May. Young hopefuls (the publicity specified boys aged 18–30, and girls of 16–25) were invited to submit applications and photographs to one of thirty Paramount representatives scattered throughout the United States. From these, the company would begin the weeding-out process, ending with a projected class of twenty students—ten boys and ten girls. It was announced that tuition for the term would be $500, and that the students were also expected to pay their living expenses, which would average about $25 per week. The company cautiously added, however, that it was prepared to be flexible on these terms, "as the directors realize that some young men and women possessing excellent qualifications might be unable to meet these expenses."[4]

Not surprisingly, applications immediately began to pour in by the thousands. Each of the thirty Paramount branch offices had been instructed to select the five most promising applications from those received, and the resulting 150 were sent to Paramount's New York office, which reduced the number by half. Ten cameramen were then dispatched to various points in the United States to make screen tests of the 75 remaining semifinalists. On the basis of these tests, 50 applicants were to be invited to New York for personal interviews, after which, at last, the final selections were to be made. But once the selection process actually began, this procedure was not rigidly followed; exceptions were made for candidates who were considered promising. In the end, fewer than half the class entered the school by the prescribed route. Some bypassed the application process altogether and were simply invited to make screen tests.

Late in July, as the dust began to settle and the school geared up for its first classes, eighteen final selections were announced.

No one was more surprised by his acceptance into the school than **Charles "Buddy" Rogers**, of Olathe, Kansas.[5] He had been studying journalism at the University of Kansas when his father, a newspaper editor in Olathe, read of the school and asked him to apply. As Rogers remembered it in later years, he was reluctant to submit an application, but did so to please his father and was invited to make a screen test. His memory of the test was ironic, in view of his later success: "Paramount sent three men there, a cameraman, an electrician, and a director. And I remember we went to the park, and there were about seven or eight of us, to make this test. I didn't have much confidence in myself; I knew I wouldn't get the part. These other boys were better. And when it came my chance they put me in front of the camera and 'All right, sing—laugh—tell a joke.' I couldn't be an actor like that!"[6] But despite his misgivings, Rogers was one of the group invited to New York and, once there, was accepted into the school. He had no acting experience whatever, but his natural talent and charisma would carry him far in the entertainment business.

Not all members of the class were even required to make screen tests; some had previous experience in films. **Greg Blackton** gained his entry through his acquaintance with William Cohill, the casting director at Astoria, who had already used him in a number of unbilled bit parts. Cohill disregarded the application requirements and simply sent Blackton for an interview with Jesse Lasky. "Cohill recommended me to him, because he had to recommend somebody," Blackton laughed, "and I happened to be there that day!"[7] Blackton's childhood had been spent in Argentina, and his speech still carried traces of an accent. He speculated that that accent, plus his appearance, established him in the faculty's minds as a "Latin" type.

Mona Palma had originally aspired to be a musician and was studying at Damrosch Institute when a commercial photographer spotted her and asked her to pose for him. This led to the beginnings of a career as a fashion model. In 1925 *Excella* magazine, in cooperation with Paramount, had conducted a contest for aspiring players who wanted to get into the movies. The two winners, May Betteridge and Florence M. Vandiver, were to appear in Paramount's remake of *Polly of the Circus*. The contest must have been jinxed: *Excella* went out of business even before the contest ended, Paramount's *Polly of the Circus* was not produced, and May Betteridge and Florence Vandiver disappeared into obscurity. But Mona had been the first runner-up, and when the Paramount school was announced, company executives remembered her and invited her to make a test—which was successful.

Another student who entered the running at the screen-test stage was **Marian Ivy Harris** (also known simply as Ivy Harris). She originally had no intention of applying for the school, but when Paramount's camera crew arrived in her native Atlanta to make tests, she was championed by a local newspaperman and accepted on the basis of the resulting test. Her natural ability and appeal were such that she would eventually be selected to play the feminine lead in the class film. (She should not be confused with the singer Marion Harris, who was more or less a contemporary, and who did appear later in sound films for MGM.)

For **Josephine Dunn**, bypassing the original application rules was nothing new; she had the kind of beauty-queen looks that naturally opened doors for her. She arrived in the school fresh from the stage chorus of *Kid Boots*, and the story was that she had started her musical-comedy experience as a teenager, simply by accompanying a friend to an audition at the Winter Garden. The friend was rejected, while Josephine was invited to join the chorus. Later, when her cousin won a screen test for the Paramount school, Josephine went along, and the same thing happened again.[8] For a time her future in films looked very bright indeed.

One bona fide beauty-contest winner, whose looks likewise propelled her into the school, was **Ethelda** (aka Thelda) **Kenvin**. As Miss Brooklyn in the 1923 Atlantic City Beauty Pageant, she had been runner-up for the title of Miss America. Next she had become a model and was working for such distinguished illustrators as Howard Chandler Christy and James Montgomery Flagg when she was approached about entering the school. Again, she was simply invited to join—and, reportedly, made her decision on the flip of a coin![9]

Thelma Todd, too, qualified as a beauty-contest winner; she had just been chosen Miss Massachusetts. But like Buddy Rogers, she entered the school from well outside the mainstream of show business—she was working as a schoolteacher in Lawrence, Massachusetts—and followed the application guidelines to the letter. She and Rogers were among the few class members who did so and, coincidentally, they would ultimately achieve greater success in the film business than any of the other class members. In 1925, however, few would have made such a prediction for Thelma. Whether through shyness or inexperience, she was rather consistently overshadowed by the other girls in press coverage, and it would be several years before she came into full flower on the screen.

For a beginner, **Robert Andrews** had substantial experience in the movies. He had begun doing extra work years earlier and had worked his way up to featured juvenile roles (one of them in the 1924 Fox remake of Lasky's *The Warrens of Virginia*) when he was hired as an assistant director. At the time of his entry into the school, he was working more behind the camera than before it, and this would be true of most of his subsequent work as well. During the term of the school he was made "student assistant."

Charles Brokaw, too, had a good deal of acting experience—but on the stage. He had established himself long since as a theatrical player; he was working steadily as a member of Jane Cowl's company. (As recently as January 1925 he had played Broadway in a small role in her production of Hans Mueller's *The Depths*.) A graduate of Ohio State University and, at 26, the oldest student in the school, Brokaw was elected president of the class.

With no acting experience at all, **Walter Goss** was one of those invited to make screen tests simply on the basis of appearance. He was working for the *New York Herald Tribune* when, according to Paramount publicity, a company scout spotted him in the audience at a Broadway theater and asked him to submit photographs. Goss would later parlay that chance occurrence into a respectable career.

Another student with a newspaper background was **Irving Hartley**, who had been a photographer for the *New York World*. Studio publicity related the story that when the *World* sent him to photograph Dorothy Gish, who was sailing for Europe, she had advised him to go into the movies.[10] Taking her advice, he became a member of the MGM stock company and got a modicum of film exposure between 1923 and 1925, which, ironically, was more than he would achieve through his place in the Paramount school.

In childhood and in military school, **Jack Luden** had been interested not in acting but in athletics. He had been a star athlete at the New York Military Academy at Cornwall-on-Hudson, but had broken his leg during the 1919 Olympic trials, forcing him to curtail his athletic career. Still, his physical conditioning enabled him to obtain stunt work in films, and he was already known at Paramount when the opportunity came to audition for the school. His would be one of the strangest and most colorful careers of any of the Paramount students.

Claud Buchanan had studied medicine for a time at Tufts College, but had succumbed to the lure of show business, and for three years had been trying to gain a foothold simultaneously in musical comedy, vaudeville, drama, and films. He claimed to have given up his first offer of a good part in order to accept a place in the school.[11]

Because of the fear that the school's tuition fee might be an obstacle to some promising candidates, the *Boston Post* made an agreement with Famous Players-Lasky to give some New England applicants a break. Within two weeks of the first public announcement of the school, the *Post* announced that it would award two "scholarships" to deserving candidates. Applicants for the scholarships were required to be residents of one of the New England states and were asked to complete a questionnaire and submit three photographs, which would then be examined by Paramount representatives. The final selection was left entirely in Paramount's hands, and to the two lucky winners, the *Post* promised to pay all tuition, travel, and living expenses.[12] From the thousands of applications received, 278 semifinalists were selected for personal interviews, the girls outnumbering the boys by nearly two to one.[13] In the end, both the scholarships were given to Massachusetts girls. **Dorothy Nourse**, of Roxbury, was at 16 the youngest member of the Paramount class. She had won some minor beauty contests, but her sole show-business experience up to this time had been a place in the chorus of Earl Carroll's *Vanities* when that production played Boston. At the time of her acceptance into the school, she was working as a clerk in a Boston department store. **Harriet Krauth**, of Medford Hillside, had likewise appeared in the Boston edition of the *Vanities*, but had manifested an early interest in the movies as well. Born in Port of Spain, Trinidad, she had been in her early teens when her family moved to Massachusetts. There she had joined a Boston movie club called the Little Screen Players, and when the club produced its own two-reel comedy, she had been the leading lady.

To these fifteen names, the original class roster added three more: Lorraine Eason, Wilbur Dillon, and Laverne Lindsay, all from Hollywood, California. But within a few weeks, these three residents of the film capital were out of the school. Why? Two years later, one magazine writer would allege without mentioning names that the three had rebelled against the school's discipline.[14] The film industry as a whole was attempting to clean up its image in the wake of the disastrous scandals of the early 1920s, and Paramount officials were well aware that they were taking impressionable boys and girls, many of them from quiet, sheltered backgrounds, and tossing them abruptly into a glamorous life filled with temptation. Accordingly, they were taking no chances. The students were closely supervised throughout the term of the school, and were required to observe a strict curfew six nights a week. When not in class, the girls were supplied with a chaperone, Mrs. J. Walter Taylor, a painter's widow. In addition, all the students who were not already New York residents were quartered in separate hotels: the Allerton Hotel for Women at 57th Street and Lexington Avenue, and the Allerton Hotel for Men at 66th Street and Madison Avenue. "We'd take the Elevated over every day and every night," said Buddy Rogers. "I remember I thought it was so funny—'Well, goodbye,' and you'd get off at a different station." It may be that the "Hollywood three" were unable to adjust to this regimented lifestyle and were promptly dismissed from the class.

But Greg Blackton remembered the situation differently. "These were three people who were in the business before," he recalled, "and they were very high-class. So they looked around at this bunch of so-called ham actors and said, 'We don't want to be with that bunch!'" He chuckled at the memory. "They left on their own, they weren't fired."[15]

Whatever the reason, the three Hollywood entries in the original class were gone by the time the serious routine of classes started. In their place was the final member of the graduating class, a Kansas girl named Berniece Leu, who had already taken the professional name of **Iris Gray**. Iris had been pursuing a career as a dancer for some time, had worked with the Denishawn company in Los Angeles, and had toured the Orpheum circuit. She was in New York in connection with her dancing career when the 1925 Paramount/*Excella* contest was announced, and at the urging of Walter Burgess, manager of the Roseland Ballroom, submitted an entry. Along with Mona Palma, she was a runner-up in the contest. When the departure of the three Hollywood students created a vacancy in the school, Iris was admitted in their place and was quickly accepted as one of the group.

With the membership of the class established, the actual training sessions began on Monday, 20 July 1925. The school's curriculum had been divided into three broad categories: technical instruction, physical training, and lectures. The physical training took the form of swimming lessons, calisthenics, and other forms of general exercise. At times the group was divided and the girls were instructed in "aesthetic dancing," while the boys were drilled in boxing or fencing. The lectures took place

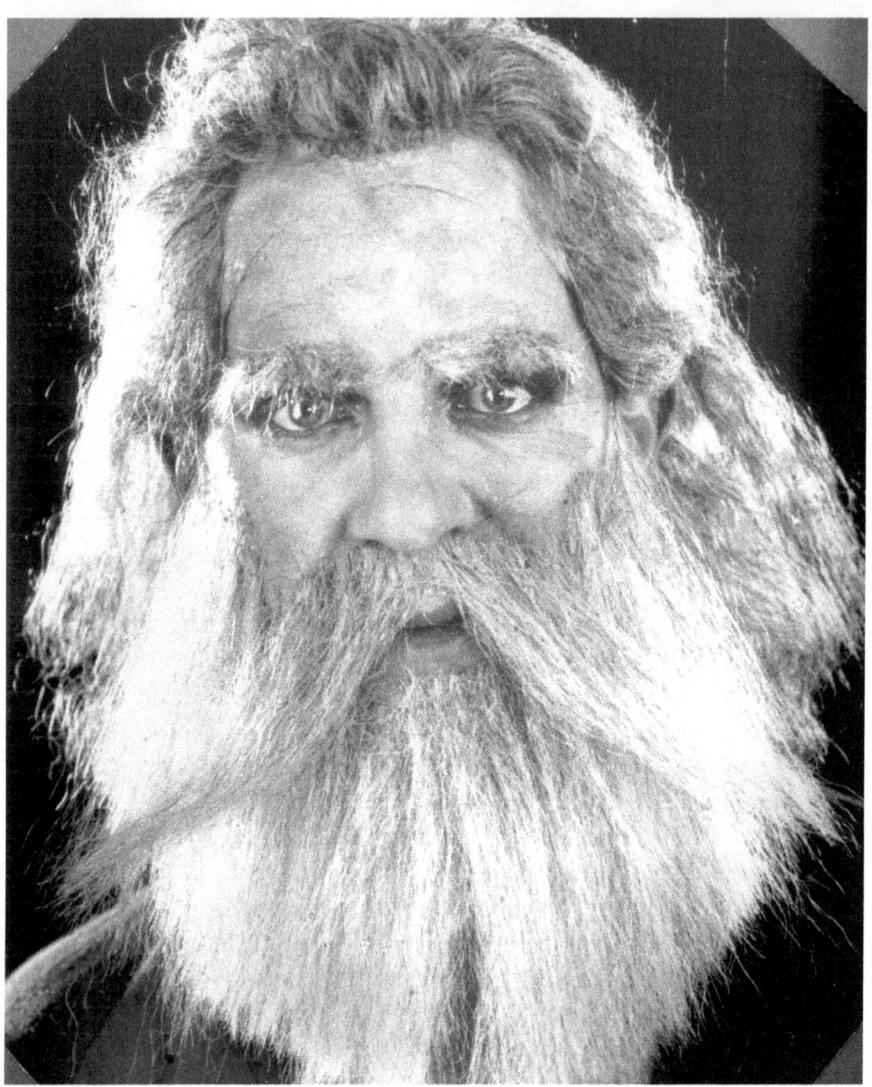

Greg Blackton, age 25, demonstrates a character makeup designed under the supervision of instructor Hal Clarendon. Courtesy Greg Blackton.

at sporadic intervals and covered subjects outside the scope of the actor's craft, such as lighting and photography.

It was, clearly, the technical instruction that formed the core of the school's curriculum. Here the students were taught the proper way to sit, stand, open a door, and all the other details that would go into a normal screen performance, leading to more extensive training in the fine points of pantomime, makeup, and costuming. A typical school day would begin at 9:30 a.m. with a period of such instruction, followed at 11:00 by a two-hour period of physical training. Some idea of the scope of the lessons may be gained by a look at the school's faculty. The physical training was in the hands of John G. Toomey, general exercise and gymnastics; Frank E. Dalton, swimming; Marcel Cabijos, fencing; and Mme. E. Grandona, dancing. George Currie, of the American Academy of Dramatic Art, instructed the students in pantomime, Virginia Terhune Van de Water in etiquette. A good deal of attention was given to costuming: H.M.K. Smith taught modern attire; Morgia Lytton, period costumes; and Hal Clarendon, period costume and makeup. And one major oversight in the original faculty roster was rectified before the end of the term by the addition of Mlle. La Sylphe—Charleston instructor.[16] In later years, both Greg Blackton and Buddy Rogers remembered the classes with some amusement. "I remember, as I look back now, they would teach us how to roll down stairs without hurting ourselves," said Rogers. "They'd teach us how to put on false beards and all that. The thing I enjoyed the most was learning how to hold a kiss for three minutes without laughing!"

The opening of the school had attracted considerable attention in the press, but as the routine of classes continued without incident, little more was heard by the public until near the end of the term. Jack Luden did attract a flurry of publicity in October 1925 when his family connection with the Luden Candy and Cough Drop Company became known.[17] (At that time, and for some time afterward, it was incorrectly claimed that he was the son of the company founder. In fact he was the founder's *nephew*, and had no other connection with the company.)

Almost from the beginning of the term, however, Paramount executives had pegged Buddy Rogers as the boy most likely. Journalists and onlookers agreed: Buddy projected a winning personality that seemed to set him apart from the rest.[18] But the question was whether he could project that personality on screen, and, unlike some of the other students, he had never appeared in a film. The decision was made to test him in a small role in a Paramount feature. "I was in the school one day," Rogers recalled, "and Mr. Lasky called me up to his office. He said, 'Buddy, do you have any knickers and argyles?' I said, 'Sure, that's all I wore at the University of Kansas.' He said, 'Wear them tomorrow when you come to the school, will you?' I said, 'Yeah.' And about ten o'clock the next morning—'Mr. Rogers, come out of the class.' I had my knickers on and my argyles. They put me in a limousine and started driving away! I didn't know where I was going, had no idea what I was up to. We get out to a golf course, way out on Long Island. And I see cameras, I see people and I see action. And I get out and they take me over and introduce me to the director, and the director says, 'Meet W.C. Fields!'" The director was Gregory La Cava, the film was the

Fields vehicle *So's Your Old Man* (Paramount, 1926), and Rogers played the sweetheart of Catherine "Kittens" Reichert, who was cast as Fields' daughter. As it turned out, this film, with its "test" role for Rogers, was released in October 1926—by which time Rogers was firmly ensconced in Hollywood, and *after* the film starring all sixteen class members had already been released to theaters.[19]

For the first two months of classes, the director of the school was Tom Terriss. Early in October, for unspecified reasons, he was replaced by Sam Wood.[20] Wood had already made his mark with such players as Gloria Swanson; ahead of him were such notable films as *A Night at the Opera* (MGM, 1935) and *Goodbye, Mr. Chips* (MGM, 1939).[21] To the Paramount students he brought a firm sense of discipline and the constant exhortation to strive for professional standards. Buddy Rogers remembered Wood as "nice, but tough;" his commands and criticism were always leavened with humor. During one rehearsal session, when a scene seemed to be dragging, Wood barked at the students: "Hey, what do you think you're doing—making *Ben-Hur?*"[22]

One practice initiated by Terriss, which Wood continued to follow, was the filming of practice scenes. A scene would be proposed, each student or combination of students would rehearse it, and then each would perform it for the camera. In this way the students could judge their own work on the screen. "I consider these classroom demonstrations about the most valuable feature of the course," Wood told a journalist.

> The practice work of the students reaches the screen in a few hours. This enables them to correct their faults, and to improve along the lines in which they show promise. The hit-or-miss movie actor, who breaks into the game as an extra, gets no chance to see his work until months later when the picture is shown in a theater. Often, he never sees it, because the scene in which he figured may have been deleted in the cutting room.[23]

The scenes were photographed by Leo Tover, who had been designated as the school's cameraman. Tover had been working in the film industry for several years, but now, at age 23, was just getting established as a Paramount cameraman. He went on to photograph the school's class feature, and then to a distinguished career as a cameraman for Paramount, RKO, and other studios. He also formed a lasting friendship with at least one of the class members. Buddy Rogers stayed in contact with Tover after both were established in Hollywood, and two decades later, when Rogers produced the mystery *Sleep, My Love* (United Artists, 1948), he hired Tover as his director of photography.

As the students progressed under Wood's tutelage, and the term neared its end, newspaper and magazine reporters were regularly invited to the sessions. More than one commented that the students' quiet timidity, at the beginning of the term, had been replaced by a boisterous confidence and enthusiasm. Critic Rose Pelswick noted that one of the girls, whom she declined to identify, had let the school go to her head. When a fellow journalist had tried to put the young actress at ease by observing that they had met before, the latter replied wearily: "I suppose so. But I meet so many people, so many important people, that I really can't remember everyone." As Pelswick commented: "She'll get over it. She's young."[24]

This increased exposure to the public was a necessary thing, because the students were about to meet the public in a crucial and decisive way: by starring in their own motion picture. This had been part of the plan from the school's inception, and now, late in October, writer Byron Morgan was brought in to start the process of devising a story which might accommodate not only sixteen stars, but these *specific* sixteen. Greg Blackton recalled that Wood and Morgan would repair to the catwalk across the northern end of the main Astoria stage while group exercise sessions were in progress, look the students over, and confer on the screen possibilities of each.[25] By assigning the story to Morgan, Paramount was sending a clear signal as to what kind of vehicle they expected for their young players; most of the films Morgan had written were fast-paced action pictures, usually revolving around auto races. He was, like Wood, a veteran of several years with Paramount, and studio publicity made much of his earlier work with Wallace Reid. "But it's going to be pretty tough," he told Agnes Smith, "writing a story to fit sixteen stars. And when they start to cast the picture, I'm going to leave town."[26]

The story Morgan devised was a characteristically action-packed one titled *Glorious Youth*.[27] It dealt with a society boy whose girlfriend is a Greenwich Village artist, but whose father wants him to marry a wealthy girl. In order to marry the girl of his choice, the boy accepts the challenge of transforming a failing winter resort into a profitable venture. At the film's climax, he accomplishes this goal by staging a publicity-generating iceboat race, and incidentally winning it himself. Buddy Rogers was cast as the boy and Ivy Harris as the artist, while Josephine Dunn was given the relatively thankless role of the society girl. (Thelma Todd had the even more thankless role of the society girl's *sister*.) The rest of the Paramount Junior Stars (as the students had voted to call themselves[28]) were cast as friends of the leading couple. Morgan also wrote in a scene in which the boy tried to attract business by inviting movie stars to the resort, thus paving the way for cameo appearances by established Paramount stars.

The story was approved and designated as production number F-311, and *Glorious Youth* went before the cameras on the main Astoria stage on 23 November 1925. (The company did not get around to officially purchasing the story from Morgan until the 4th of December, by which time the film had been in production for two weeks.[29])

The Junior Stars plunged into the making of the film with zeal. "Mr. Lasky just had to let them make that picture," Agnes Smith noted. "If he hadn't, his first class in the school would have gone up in spontaneous combustion."[30] Paramount staged an interesting publicity stunt: all the film reviewers from the New York newspapers were invited to the set of *Glorious Youth* on the first day of production. There they were encouraged to meet and chat with the students—a situation which proved somewhat awkward until Gloria Swanson was brought in to break the ice—and to watch a scene being filmed for the picture. The scene: Charleston dancing. Then everyone adjourned to the reception room for tea.[31]

During the first four weeks of production, Iris Gray's mother was a visitor on the set. Upon her return to Wichita, Kansas, she announced to the local newspapers that she had been impressed by the environment Paramount had provided for the students:

> Every member of the school in which my daughter has graduated with honors is properly chaperoned at all times, and they are all treated with the utmost consideration. I am convinced that while there may be immoral conduct among persons in the motion picture profession, the big majority are moral and rank well up with, or in advance of other professions.[32]

The studio shooting of *Glorious Youth* was completed on 24 December 1925, and the students were given a short break for Christmas. On Monday, 28 December, they were taken by train to Lake Placid, in upper New York state, to begin shooting exteriors, an event which, as Greg Blackton remembered it, was marked by several cases of frostbite:

> We got off the train and we were dressed like we were in New York. But it was a very cold day, and quite a few of us, our ears were frostbitten. So we went to the Lake Placid Club, a very exclusive place. We were guests there for the duration. And for two or three days we didn't film at all. There were about four boys, and about three or four girls, that were laid up until they just got well enough to go outside and shoot some film.

The company was quartered in Onondaga Cottage for a stay that lasted about three weeks. The management and guests of Lake Placid

On location in Red Bank, New Jersey, for the filming of the iceboat race, four of the Junior Stars pose for a publicity photo. Left to right: Iris Gray, Dorothy Nourse, Ivy Harris, and Jeanne Morgan.

Club were delighted to have the Paramount group with them, the more so when Richard Dix, Adolphe Menjou, Clara Bow, Lois Wilson, and other Paramount stars arrived to make their cameo appearances in the film. A number of guests of the club appeared in the film as extras, and one guest, champion ski jumper Hans Troye of Oslo, performed his specialty for the camera. The company also shot some professional "home movies" of the club's regular activities and presented them to the club as a gift in return for the latter's hospitality.[33] From Lake Placid, the company went to the North Shrewsbury River near Red Bank, New Jersey, to shoot the scenes of the iceboat race.

During the closing weeks of production, all sixteen of the Junior Stars were notified that they would be given one-year contracts with Paramount. This was a relief to most of them, for until that time none of them had been guaranteed a job with Paramount, or any other studio, when the classes were over. All had signed temporary contracts covering their appearance in *Glorious Youth*,[34] which gave Paramount the *option* of signing each of them within two weeks after the end of production, but no promises were made until February 1926. The one-year contract provided a salary of $75 a week for the first six months and $100 a week for the second six months, and also included five options. If the company exercised all its options, the student would be a Paramount player for five years, at the end of which time he or she would be earning $500 per week. As soon as *Glorious Youth* had finished shooting, company executives, convinced that Buddy Rogers was a genuine find, wasted no time in rushing him to Hollywood, where he was promised a major role in *Beau Geste*. (That role failed to materialize, as did a subsequently promised one in *Old Ironsides*; but then, of course, he was given the lead in *Wings*.) The rest of the students were advised to take a short rest until the first of March, when their tenure as Paramount stock players officially began.[35]

Sometime during the latter half of the school's session, Harriet Krauth had made the decision to change her professional name to Jeanne Morgan (see Table 1). After the end of production on the students' film, another name change took place: the title of the film was changed from *Glorious Youth* to *Fascinating Youth*. No official reason was offered for the change, but one wag suggested that Gloria Swanson, then reigning at Paramount, was afraid the original title might be misunderstood as "Gloria's Youth."[36]

The "graduation" ceremony of the Paramount Pictures School was a gala affair held at the Ritz-Carlton Hotel on 2 March 1926. Buddy Rogers was brought back from California for the occasion, and he and the other Junior Stars flanked Jesse Lasky at the speaker's table, presiding over an invited audience of 300, many of whom were, of course, representatives of the press. Dinner was served, after which Lasky made a short speech largely paraphrased from his press release the previous April when the school was first announced. (His speech was also printed in the graduation program.) Charles Brokaw, the class president, responded with a speech of his own in which he thanked Lasky for his encouragement and support, and then, on behalf of the class, presented him with a gold cigarette case. Undoubtedly the highlight of the evening, as far as the students were concerned, was the presentation of "diplomas:" their signed contracts.

For most of those in attendance, however, the highlight was the first public screening of *Fascinating Youth*. (The feature was accompanied by a short selection of clips, made during the early months of the school, which illustrated the progress the students had made in the meantime.) The feature aroused a generally favorable response. As *Photoplay* put it: "Nobody expected the picture to be much good and everybody was agreeably disappointed."[37] Dorothy Herzog of the *Mirror* agreed: "Those who came to laugh remained to admire, for this flicker, while slight in story, vibrates with youthful buoyancy, delightful comedy touches, romance, and a snappy climax."[38] Regina Cannon of the *Graphic* joined in, claiming that this class project was "a production that Paramount may be proud to release."[39]

But even such qualified praise was not unanimous. *Motion Picture* called the film "pert, flippant, shallow and rather futile entertainment"

Table 1: Students in the Paramount School
Names of Paramount students, in the form of the three lists that appeared in the *New York Times* at the beginning of the term (21 July 1925), at the midpoint (18 October 1925), and at the time of graduation (7 March 1926). They are arranged in corresponding columns, each headed by a citation indicating the article's appearance in the *Times*. This should help to clarify the changes of name and personnel that took place during that period. Some spelling changes are probably not significant, but all are preserved anyway for the sake of accuracy.

21 July 1925 (26:3)	18 October 1925 (IX:5:4–5:7)	7 March 1926 (VIII:5:3)
Robert Andrews	Robert Andrews	Robert Andrews
Greg Blackton	Greg Blackton	Greg Blackton
Charles Brokaw	Charles Brokaw	Charles Brokaw
Claud Buchanan	Claud Buchanan	Claude Buchanan
Josephine Dunn	Josephine Dunn	Josephine Dunn
Walter J. Goss	Walter Goss	Walter Goss
Marian Ivy Harris	Marian Ivy Harris	Ivy Harris
Irving Hartley	Irving Hartley	Irving Hartley
Ethelda Kenvin	Ethelda Kenvin	Thelda Kenvin
Harriet Krauth	Harriet Krauth	Jeanne Morgan
John Luden	Jack Luden	Jack Luden
Dorothy Nourse	Dorothy Nourse	Dorothy Nourse
Mona Palma	Mona Palma	Mona Palma
Charles Rogers	Charles Rogers	Charles Rogers
Thelma Todd	Thelma Todd	Thelma Todd
	Iris Grey	Iris Gray
Wilbur Dillon		
Lorraine Eason		
Laverne Lindsay		

and declared that "none of the sixteen pupils shows any sign of causing the Atlantic Ocean to burst into flames." While grudgingly acknowledging that Buddy Rogers seemed to have possibilities, the reviewer complained that most of the girls were overweight, and added that "these debutantes seem a little bit hard, cocky and sure of themselves, compared with regular actresses of the screen."[40] *Motion Picture Classic* opined that "One thing is proved clearly: it isn't possible to turn out players this way." But this opinion was balanced by Richard Dix's candid admission, overheard at the graduation dinner, that "I wouldn't have lasted a week at the school. I can swim but I can't fall down with any sort of grace. I can't fence, I'm a rotten dancer and what I don't know about etiquette would fill a book. I certainly was lucky to land in pictures before they started schools!"[41] As the picture began to appear in regular theatrical engagements, the division of critical opinion continued. The general consensus seemed to be that the film was pretty good, but that its light, enjoyable plot and fast-paced direction would have saved it, no matter who was in the cast. Much critical attention was reserved for James Bradbury, Sr. in the comedy role of a gouty old professor.

Variety, characteristically, got right to the point: "Here is a picture that has exploitation values if any picture had them . . . The box office appeal of the production will be big in the cities where the graduates hail from."[42] This was the publicity angle upon which Paramount was banking: the public's interest in the Junior Stars themselves. The whole idea of the school—taking young unknowns and turning them into professional movie players in a few months—had a special intrigue about it, and company executives were staking their hopes on the public's interest in seeing the results. To capitalize on any such interest, *Fascinating Youth* was mounted as a road show, with a stage prologue in which the Junior Stars appeared in person before the film was shown. Paramount lavished special attention on this stage show; the distinguished producer of stage revues, John Murray Anderson, was brought in to prepare the presentation.[43] Assisted by Glenn Alvine of Famous Players, he concocted a miniature musical show built around the school itself. This piqued public interest in the whole Junior Stars phenomenon, and also gave the students with stage experience, especially the girls who had been dancers, a chance to further display that training. The process of making movies was genially lampooned, and at one point in the proceedings, Greg Blackton and Thelma Todd danced a tango. The stage show was first announced as "Getting Into the Movies,"[44] but thereafter was generally referred to as "Alice in Movieland."

The three-month tour of *Fascinating Youth*, complete with stage prologue, began on 9 May 1926 at the Rivoli Theatre in New York. Only twelve of the sixteen students appeared on stage; Buddy Rogers was

Table 2: Itinerary of the *Fascinating Youth* Tour

Based on a schedule that was published before the start of the tour by *Exhibitors Daily Review*, 9 April 1926, p. 1, and modified by changes of date that are known to have been made during the course of the tour.

Opening date	City	Theater
9 May 1926	New York	Rivoli
16 May	Boston	Metropolitan
23 May	Buffalo	Shea's Buffalo
30 May	Detroit	Capitol
6 June	Chicago	Chicago
13 June	Chicago	Tivoli
20 June (5-day layoff)*	Chicago	Uptown
3 July	St. Louis	Missouri
10 July	Kansas City	Newman
18 July	Dallas	Palace
25 July	Memphis	Loew's Palace
1 August	Atlanta	Howard

* Although Wichita, Kansas was not officially part of the tour, Iris Gray and Greg Blackton (and *Fascinating Youth*) made an appearance at the Miller Theater there on 28–30 June.

already back in Hollywood, and Mona Palma, Walter Goss, and Jack Luden apparently were working before the cameras as well. The show was a popular success during its week at the Rivoli, whereupon it moved to Boston, the home base for Thelma Todd, Jeanne Morgan, Dorothy Nourse, and Claud Buchanan. The tour was set up as a series of one-week engagements at selected Paramount Publix theaters; the show would usually play a theater from Sunday through Saturday, then move to the next engagement and begin again on Sunday (see Table 2). From Boston the company went to Buffalo, then headed west. In Chicago they stayed for three weeks at three different theaters. At the end of the third week an extra day was added, because the students were about to take a five-day break, and their engagement in St. Louis did not begin until the next weekend.

At this point, Iris Gray paid a visit to her hometown. It had been decided that, even though Wichita was excluded from the tour, Iris Gray and Greg Blackton might appear there during the break in the schedule.

While on tour in Memphis, eleven of the Paramount Junior Stars pose for a group picture. Seated at the left of the desk is Buddy Rogers; seated at the right is Greg Blackton. Standing, left to right, are Irving Hartley, Charles Brokaw, Iris Gray, Thelda Kenvin, Robert Andrews, Ivy Harris, Dorothy Nourse, Josephine Dunn, and Thelma Todd. Courtesy Greg Blackton.

But the date scheduled for their first appearance was Monday, 28 June, and when the company's extra day in Chicago was added, Iris and Blackton were left with less than a day to get from Chicago to Wichita. Not to be defeated, Wichita's Miller Theater staged a stunt that allowed the show to go on as scheduled and provided the tour with good news copy at the same time. At the end of the last show in Chicago on the 27th, the two Junior Stars walked off the stage of the Uptown Theater and into a taxi which whisked them to the railroad station, where they caught the last train to Kansas City. At 10:30 the next morning the train arrived in Kansas City, where a special car was waiting to rush them to Richards Air Field, 14 miles away. Arrangements had been made with the Travel Air Company, and pilot C.E. Clark was waiting at Richards Field with his plane warmed up and ready to go. After a quick pause for photographs, the two young celebrities boarded the plane and were in the air by 11:20. Arriving at the Wichita Municipal Airport at 2:05 p.m., they were met by another car, which got them to the Miller just in time for their 2:30 stage appearance! That show was followed by two more the same day, one of them attended by C.A. Rogers, Buddy's father, who had driven 200 miles from Olathe. His home was only a few miles from Kansas City, but the film was not scheduled there until two weeks later, and Rogers announced that he couldn't wait that long. When theater management discovered who he was, he was treated royally and taken backstage to meet his son's classmates. The two young players continued their run at the Miller for two more days, during which time they were both guests of Iris' family. At the end of the week they boarded another train, the Sunflower, and rejoined the rest of the troupe in St. Louis to resume the tour. The company worked its way through the Midwest and then back through the South, ending with an appearance in Atlanta, Ivy Harris' hometown.

Along the way, in addition to their stage performances, the Junior Stars engaged in public-relations activities that helped to establish them as familiar names. In Buffalo they were loaned three large Gardner cars, in which they were given a sightseeing tour of the city. In Boston, Josephine Dunn, Iris Gray, and Thelda Kenvin were escorted through police headquarters, where they were shown, among other things, confiscated weapons, drug paraphernalia, and moonshine and, according to the press, "left delighted with their sightseeing expedition."[45] Other members of the troupe made occasional radio broadcasts or endorsed products.

In Kansas City, the leg of the tour nearest Buddy Rogers' hometown, Rogers rejoined the group for a week of appearances and special activities. On Saturday, 10 July, they paid a visit to the children at Mercy Hospital, signing autographs and doing impromptu musical performances. The following Monday and Tuesday they stood in as "guest clerks" at Woolf Brothers department store, waiting on customers and selling hosiery and handkerchiefs. "Of course," the newspapers explained, "every now and then some pretty girl or attractive young chap, permanently attached to Woolf's sales force, was pointed out by one customer to another as 'Iris Gray' or 'Claud Buchanan.' But neither the regular employee nor his temporary substitute seemed to mind, and the visitors, who were thrilled by their sight of a 'real motion picture star,' didn't know the difference."[46]

After the concluding performance of the tour, on 7 August 1926 in Atlanta, the Junior Stars returned to New York. (*Fascinating Youth* went into standard theatrical release later the same month, and eventually realized a modest profit.[47]) No sooner had they returned than Thelma Todd was stricken with appendicitis and rushed back to a hospital in Lawrence, Massachusetts. As if that were not enough, most of the group were discovering that the end of the tour brought with it an uncertain future. Those one-year contracts were actually designed to allow Paramount the option of reviewing each player's performance at three-month intervals, and dropping those who didn't appear satisfactory. This meant that the Junior Stars were on far less stable ground than they had imagined. After all, *Fascinating Youth*, and the Junior Stars as a group, had both been fairly well received, but most of the group were still unknown quantities as individual players, and at first Paramount was unsure how to use them. They had, as a rule, been chosen on the basis of their looks, not their histrionic ability. Consequently, most of them turned up within the first year as "window dressing" in Paramount features; whenever a good-looking boy or girl was needed in a scene, the studio could always fall back on one of the Junior Stars. Following Buddy Rogers' lead, Ivy Harris, Claud Buchanan, Jack Luden, and Josephine Dunn appeared as juveniles in W.C. Fields features, while Thelma Todd and Robert Andrews managed somewhat more substantial roles in Ed Wynn's *Rubber Heels* (1927). D.W. Griffith effected his only real contact with the school by using Dorothy Nourse, Jeanne Morgan, and Josephine Dunn in a quick appearance in *The Sorrows of Satan* (1926).

Paramount had originally announced that *Fascinating Youth* would be followed by three more films featuring the entire student body of the school,[48] which should have given each of the sixteen ample time to prove him- or herself. But as early as July 1926, while the tour was still in progress, *Exhibitors Trade Review* reported that the second class film was "entirely in the air, with no one volunteering any information about it."[49] In the end, the film was not produced; instead, members of the class began to be dropped from the Paramount ranks. The first three-month review period had ended in the midst of the *Fascinating Youth* tour, so of course all the Junior Stars were retained. But the second period closed at the end of August, and at that point Paramount began to let some of them go. Before the end of October, the original sixteen had been reduced to six: Buddy Rogers, Jack Luden, Walter Goss, Mona Palma, Thelma Todd, and Iris Gray.[50] Later, Ivy Harris and Josephine Dunn were restored to the list.[51] Early in 1927 it was announced that Paramount was partially reviving the idea of the class films with a new production featuring some of the surviving Junior Stars, along with other new faces who had been discovered in the interim. The script was being written by Louise Long and Ethel Doherty, and had the working title *Sheiks and Shebas*.[52] But by the time the film was released in June, it had been completely rewritten and retitled *Rolled Stockings*, and the only "new face" featured in it was supporting player Nancy Phillips—a fact which did not prevent the studio from indiscriminately advertising *all* the principals as "Paramount Junior Stars."[53] Thereafter, if any two of the original Junior Stars appeared together in the same film, it was only a coincidence.

By this time the idea of the school itself had died, too, and rather quickly at that. One of the first announcements of the *Fascinating Youth* tour had stated that a cameraman would accompany the troupe on the road, making screen tests in each city where the show was playing, and that members of the second class would be selected from those tests.[54] But no such thing occurred, and by July 1926 the trade press noted that Paramount executives had little to say about the future of the school.[55] In October the official announcement was made: the school would not be continued.[56]

Meanwhile, Buddy Rogers was fulfilling the promise he had shown in the school. After several false starts, he landed the leading role in *Wings* (Paramount, 1927), William Wellman's epic of World War aviation. This one performance was enough to establish him as a star, a status he would enjoy for years to come. Today, his two best remembered films are probably *Wings* and *My Best Girl* (Mary Pickford/United Artists, 1927), the picture that costarred him with Mary Pickford, whom he later married. But there were many other films as well; and while some of those films were, in themselves, badly received by critics, Rogers' star status never faltered. The coming of sound, before which so many film careers crumbled, posed no problem for Rogers. He spoke on the screen for the first time in *Varsity* (Paramount, 1928), a film he referred to in later years as his "voice test." His voice proved more than adequate, and he was off and running again. He had been a budding musician before his brush with the movies, playing several instruments and leading a band at Kansas University. Now Paramount found plenty of work for him in musicals: *Close Harmony* (1929) and *Follow Thru* (1930) opposite Nancy Carroll; *Heads Up* (1930) with Helen Kane; and the studio's all-star extravaganza of 1930, *Paramount on Parade*. Another notable Rogers film of this period was *Young Eagles* (Paramount, 1930), directed by William Wellman, a sound sequel to *Wings*. As the 1930s wore on, Rogers began to diversify his career, interspersing his film roles with other activities. He appeared on the Broadway stage in 1932 in Ziegfeld's *Hot-Cha!*, toured with his own band, and went behind the camera to dabble in film production. In the end, he parlayed his chance encounter with Paramount into a long and successful career.

Thelma Todd didn't hit her stride right away, but ultimately she, too, made a distinctive mark on film history. Like Rogers, she made the transition to talkies with ease, and created her own special niche in film when she signed with the Hal Roach studio. As early as the opening months of the Paramount school she had perceptively decided that her forte was comedy,[57] and in the early 1930s she proved it with a prolific string of comedy roles. Today's film enthusiast may remember her best for her appearances with the Marx Brothers in *Monkey Business* (Paramount, 1931) and *Horse Feathers* (Paramount, 1932), but she was also seen to good advantage opposite Buster Keaton (*Speak Easily*, MGM, 1932), Wheeler and Woolsey (*Hips, Hips, Hooray*; *Cockeyed Cavaliers*, both RKO, 1934), and Joe E. Brown (*Broad Minded*, First National, 1931; *Son of a Sailor*, First National, 1933). Perhaps best of all was her work at the Roach studio, appearing in shorts with Laurel and Hardy, Charley Chase, Harry Langdon, and eventually a series in which she and ZaSu Pitts (and later Patsy Kelly) were teamed as the featured stars. Occasionally, as in *Horse Feathers*, she was able to display her lovely singing voice. Thelma did achieve a distinguished career and might have achieved far more than she did if not for her tragic and mysterious death in 1935.

"Half of the people in *Fascinating Youth*," said Greg Blackton, "never got to the point where they could say, 'I was a movie star.'" Actually, the figure was more than half—but then again, Buddy Rogers and Thelma Todd were not the only members of the class to find success in films. Josephine Dunn seemed at first to be headed for a long stellar career. Though Paramount had been slow to renew her contract, they used her extensively through 1927, then dropped her again. But Josephine's beauty, which had already opened so many doors for her, came to her rescue once more when MGM hired her for the feminine lead in *Excess Baggage* (1928), then signed her to a contract. During 1928–29 she was kept busy, both at MGM and on numerous loan-outs, one of which was to play opposite Al Jolson in *The Singing Fool* (Warner Bros., 1928). In 1929 she was named one of the year's Wampas Baby Stars.[58] Throughout this time, however, she was dogged by unfavorable reviews, most of which pointed out repeatedly that her acting ability was not on a par with her looks. When MGM dropped her at the end of her term, her film appearances became more and more erratic. She was reunited with Buddy Rogers in 1930 in Paramount's *Safety in Numbers* (they had already played together in *Get Your Man*, likewise at Paramount, in 1927), and had a small role in the classic *One Hour With You* (Paramount, 1932). But as film roles became increasingly scarce, she turned back to the stage, again without great distinction. In 1935 she was announced for a little-theatre production of Samson Raphaelson's *Accent on Youth* in Shrewsbury, New Jersey, near the site where the iceboat scenes for *Fascinating Youth* had been filmed nine years earlier. The play's opening was delayed twice by labor disputes, and when it did take place Josephine was no longer in the cast. But she turned up a scant two weeks later in a production of *She Cried for the Moon* in nearby Deal.[59] By this time she was in the news more for her multiple marriages and divorces than for her work as an actress, and soon she faded from sight altogether. She lived until 1983, when she succumbed to cancer.

Jack Luden, who had kept something of a low profile in the school (once his false notoriety as the cough-drop heir had subsided), suddenly blossomed forth with a prolific career, but one which ultimately took a strange turn, and today is still shrouded in mystery. At first Paramount seemed unsure how to use him, but after he had played leads in several independent features and a series of shorts for FBO, Paramount seemed to rediscover him and cast him in a long string of featured roles and leads. Perhaps the most significant of these was *Shootin' Irons* (1927), in which, for the first time, he played the lead in a Western. But Luden's roles began to diminish in size after about a year, and his status plummeted with the coming of sound; apparently he suffered from a speech impediment. During the early years of sound, he was reduced to the level of brief supporting roles in a number of Paramount films (among them *Young Eagles*, which starred Buddy Rogers). From there he drifted into a series of bits and small roles, an obscurity broken briefly in the late 1930s by a starring role in a short-lived series of Westerns for Columbia. These low-budget productions, featuring Luden as a cowboy named "Breezy Larkin," are his best-remembered films today. The series ended after four films, but he managed to sustain his screen career until the mid-1940s. His later life was a mystery until 1987, when a fan named Luther Hathcock tracked down some information. He discovered that Luden had been sentenced to San Quentin in 1950 on charges of issuing insufficient funds (then a felony in California) and of heroin possession, and had died there in 1951, a bizarre conclusion to a story that still seems to be largely untold.[60] More than one Paramount Junior Star came to a sad end, but Jack Luden was the only one to die in prison.

After *Fascinating Youth*, Mona Palma appeared in three more films for Paramount, then abruptly vanished. But if her career was brief, it was distinguished; one of the three pictures was *The Canadian* (1926), based on Somerset Maugham's play *The Land of Promise*, and Mona essayed the central, pivotal role. Quickly forgotten, the film was rediscovered in the late 1960s by the American Film Institute and was found to be something of a precursor to Lillian Gish's better-known *The Wind* (MGM, 1928). It was praised by no less than Kevin Brownlow as "one of the most difficult kinds of pictures to make . . . Not for a moment are the performances exaggerated."[61] If only on the strength of this one film, Mona Palma left behind a noteworthy legacy.

She was not the only one of the graduates to retire with only a few credits; Ivy Harris likewise appeared in a handful of Paramount films (among them W.C. Fields' *The Potters*, 1927), then dropped out of sight. In at least one such case, a graduate of the school brought her film career to a deliberate end. Iris Gray seemed to be on the verge of considerable success; more than one critic had described her as "an exceptional find."[62] But early in 1927, she married vaudeville headliner Frank Lynch and willingly retired from the movies. "I can't help it," she told a reporter. "A happy marriage seems more worth while to me than movie fame."[63] True to her word, she settled down to a long and happy domestic career as a wife and mother, which lasted until her death in 1988.

When Paramount dropped her in the fall of 1926, Jeanne Morgan refused to accept defeat. She traveled west to Hollywood and eventually played leads in several action pictures released by FBO. The talkie revolution seemed to pose no great problem for Jeanne, with her previous experience on the musical stage, and she did find work as a chorus girl in film musicals. She joined the Busby Berkeley chorus in the film version of Eddie Cantor's *Whoopee!* (Goldwyn/United Artists, 1930), and was signed to a contract by First National. Early in 1930 she was even selected by the prominent illustrator Henry Clive as "the most beautiful show girl in Hollywood." "Hollywood show girls are the most beautiful in the world," Clive declared, "and it was a difficult task to select one of them. Yet I am sure that I have made no mistake. Miss Morgan has no rival."[64] But Jeanne's younger sister, Violet Krauth, who had come west with her, was likewise finding work as a chorus girl (under the pseudonym of Marilyn Morgan), and was likewise under contract to First National. Early in 1931, Violet/Marilyn was "discovered" by her own studio and shot to fame almost literally overnight as Marian Marsh, playing Trilby opposite John Barrymore in *Svengali*.[65] After that she enjoyed a substantial film career which lasted well into the early 1940s, and Jeanne quietly stepped aside.

The later accomplishments of one Paramount Junior Star have almost always been overlooked, because he achieved them under a changed name. Even during the closing months of the school, Walter Goss was having misgivings about his given name and announced that he intended to change it, professionally, to Robert Ward.[66] (He is, in fact, so credited in some reviews of *Fascinating Youth*.[67]) Reverting to his own name, he appeared as Walter Goss in two Paramount films, then was dropped by the studio. This must have strengthened his resolve, because he adopted the professional name of Roland Drew. Coincidentally or not, with his new name and a new mustache, he suddenly found himself in demand as a leading man. His career peaked almost immediately at the very end of the silent era, most notably when director Edwin Carewe cast him opposite Dolores del Río in *Ramona* (Inspiration/United Artists, 1928) and *Evangeline* (Edwin Carewe-Feature Productions/United Artists, 1929). Drew foundered in the early days of sound and, like so many other silent-film players, retreated to the New York and London stage to polish his speaking technique. (He never achieved any great distinction on the stage, but one of his appearances was in the Broadway run of Sidney Howard's *Paths of Glory*.) He staged a moderately successful screen comeback in 1937, and for years thereafter was seen in a variety of character roles, particularly during a busy stint as a Warner Bros. contract player in 1941–42. Drew's Warners credits included a minor role in *Across the Pacific* (1942), but perhaps the most interesting of his later appearances were the leading role in PRC's *Beasts of Berlin* (1939), an anti-Nazi propaganda film, and the role of King Barin of Vulcan in the last of Universal's "Flash Gordon" serials (*Flash Gordon Conquers the Universe*, 1940). In the late 1940s, he retired from acting and entered the garment industry. He died in 1988.

The experience of the Paramount school apparently turned at least one of its students *away* from the movies. No sooner had the *Fascinating Youth* tour concluded than Charles Brokaw went back to the stage and Jane Cowl. By early 1927, he was appearing in her Broadway production of Robert Sherwood's *The Road to Rome*. Brokaw remained a stage actor until the late 1930s, when he accepted some roles in minor films like Universal's *I Cover the War* (1937), and even then returned to the theatre periodically. He never achieved great celebrity in either theatre or film, but kept his acting career going at least as late as the 1940s. He died in 1975.

Why did the school fail? The Paramount executives can hardly be blamed for their reluctance to continue the project. The results, at the time, did not seem to justify the effort and expense involved. As matters stood in late 1926, the studio had one sure find, Buddy Rogers, and fifteen unknown quantities—hardly a promising average. But with so much going for it, why hadn't the school itself succeeded? One journalist, writing in 1927, argued that no classroom instruction, however expert, could take the place of practical experience. "Throwing a bunch of amateurs together will not develop each one nearly as well as putting each individual amongst a group of experienced professionals," Charles Paton explained. "In fact, it is quite probable that the actual graduates of the School learned far more in the six months of hanging about the studio [after the end of classes], and making the best of whatever was tossed their way, than they did during the whole existence of the School proper."[68]

Jesse Lasky, writing his autobiography three decades after the fact, had a different explanation:

What I had failed to take into consideration was that looks and talent and training aren't enough by themselves. More important than all three is personality—and that's something you can't turn out by factory methods. To be sure, Buddy and Thelma benefited amazingly from the school, but they had personality galore, and untapped dramatic ability as well, before they came to us, or they would never have landed on top.[69]

Whatever the reasons, the school had failed to justify itself in Paramount's eyes, and its doors were closed forever. The studio continued to try various training programs for the players it already had under contract—and Lasky hatched the occasional new scheme like his "Gateway to Hollywood" radio program—but nothing quite like the Paramount Pictures School was ever attempted again. From today's perspective, that seems a shame. The school offered the romantic prospect of a modern Cinderella story, taking an absolute unknown and boosting him or her to the heights of movie stardom, and, in at least one case, such a story actually did come to pass. In the long run, too, there were practical benefits. American film history would be poorer without the contributions of Buddy Rogers and Thelma Todd, and, to a lesser degree, Jack Luden, Josephine Dunn, Roland Drew, and Mona Palma—not to mention Marian Marsh, whose break in the movies surely owed something to her sister's. We have the Paramount school to thank for all these familiar faces, and we can only wonder how many others might have brightened our screens if the school had continued.

Notes

1. "Establish National School for Screen Acting," *New York Times*, 5 April 1925, IX:5:6.
2. Ibid.
3. "The First Real School of Screen Acting," *Photoplay*, May 1925, p. 68.
4. "Form School to Train New Movie Actors," *New York Times*, 1 April 1925, 21:1.
5. Pronounced o-lay-the (soft *th*). The name of the town has sometimes been misspelled "Olante" in accounts of Rogers' career.
6. This and subsequent quotes, Charles "Buddy" Rogers to author, 18 May 1987 and 20 February 1989.
7. This and subsequent quotes, Greg Blackton to author, 4 April 1989 and 27 June 1989. Greg Blackton, incidentally, was no relation to J. Stuart Blackton.
8. See W. Adolphe Roberts, "Training Tomorrow's Screen Stars," *Everybody's Magazine*, February 1926, pp. 72–73.
9. This story was related in both "Sixteen Lucky Students," *New York Times* (18 October 1925, IX:5:6), and the school's graduation program (2 March 1926).
10. "Sixteen Lucky Students," *New York Times*, 18 October 1925, IX:5:7; and the school's graduation program, 2 March 1926.
11. Ibid.
12. "Post to Give Movie School Scholarships," *Boston Post*, 13 April 1925, pp. 1, 11.
13. "Here's First List of Movie Choices," *Boston Post*, 31 May 1925, pp. 1, 30.
14. Charles Paton, "School is Dismissed," *Motion Picture Classic*, June 1927, p. 33.
15. Easily the most experienced of the three was Lorraine Eason, who had played leads in a number of independent productions for Richard Talmadge and others. Whatever the circumstances of her departure from the school, they did not prevent her from appearing late in 1926 in a West Coast-produced Paramount film, *We're in the Navy Now*. The film was a Wallace Beery-Raymond Hatton vehicle, and Lorraine's was a "window dressing" role, not unlike those that some of the school's graduates were playing around the same time. As for Laverne Lindsay, she was relatively inexperienced in 1925, but shortly thereafter she adopted the professional name of Sharon Lynn, and ultimately achieved a substantial film career even without the benefit of the school.
16. This list is the combined result of two published accounts, from the beginning and end of the term: *New York Times*, 21 July 1925, 26:3, and the school's graduation program, 2 March 1926. Morgia Lytton's name, in the first list, is replaced by that of Mrs. Frederick Loomis in the second. Could they both have been the same person?
17. "Jack Luden Pupil in a Movie School," *New York Times*, 6 October 1925, 30:3.
18. W. Adolphe Roberts, "Training Tomorrow's Screen Stars," *Everybody's Magazine*, February 1926, p. 72; Katherine Zimmerman, "Screen Cubs," *Photoplay*, May 1926, p. 64, for examples.
19. This raises some question as to the accuracy of Rogers' account, since production of *So's Your Old Man* didn't take place until the spring of 1926. (During the actual term of the school, Fields was primarily occupied with

shooting D.W. Griffith's *That Royle Girl*; see "It Was Always Funny Working with Fields," elsewhere in this volume.) Certainly it would not be surprising if Rogers suffered a faulty memory of the events of sixty years earlier. On the other hand, he does appear in *So's Your Old Man*, in a minor "window dressing" role that would have been unlikely by the time of *Wings*, and the film was produced at Paramount's Astoria studio. In light of these circumstances I have elected to let Rogers' statement stand without challenge.

20. This action may have been prompted by a contract dispute. Both before and after his tenure with the school, Terriss directed films for companies other than Paramount (although a couple of his earlier Cosmopolitan productions were *released* by Paramount), while Wood had been a prolific Paramount director for five years.
21. But see "Random Thoughts on the 'Best Picture' vs. the 'Best Director'," p. 598, for a sobering reappraisal of Wood's talent by William K. Everson.
22. Reported by Agnes Smith, "Waiting for the Starlight," *Photoplay*, December 1925, p. 131. By this time, of course, MGM's gargantuan production of *Ben-Hur* had been dragging on for a good two years. See Kevin Brownlow, *The Parade's Gone By . . .*, chapter 36, "The Heroic Fiasco: *Ben-Hur*."
23. Sam Wood quoted by W. Adolphe Roberts in "Training Tomorrow's Screen Stars," *Everybody's Magazine*, February 1926, p. 75.
24. Rose Pelswick in an unidentified clipping, Iris Gray scrapbook.
25. See Richard Koszarski, *The Astoria Studio and Its Fabulous Films*, pp. 7–8.
26. Byron Morgan quoted by Agnes Smith in "Waiting for the Starlight," *Photoplay*, December 1925, p. 53.
27. The year before, Morgan had furnished the original story for Universal's *Sporting Youth*.
28. W. Adolphe Roberts, "Training Tomorrow's Screen Stars," *Everybody's Magazine*, February 1926, p. 74. The label was subsequently adopted and used by the company.
29. Paramount script file, *Fascinating Youth*. Paramount collection, Margaret Herrick Library, Academy of Motion Picture Arts and Sciences (hereinafter identified as "AMPAS").
30. Agnes Smith, "Waiting for the Starlight," *Photoplay*, December 1925, p. 53.
31. Reported by Helen Klumph, "Helen Looks Over the Budding Stars," *New York Morning Telegraph*, 29 November 1925. This was apparently the scene of the incident described above by Rose Pelswick.
32. Mrs. Fred Leu quoted in unidentified Wichita clipping, Iris Gray scrapbook. Of course, no one actually "graduated" from the school until later.
33. Unidentified Lake Placid clipping, Iris Gray scrapbook.
34. Temporary contract form dated 10 November 1925, about two weeks before the start of production.
35. Letter from Jesse Lasky to students, February 1926.

36. Katherine Zimmerman, "Pets of Paramount," *New York Telegram*, undated clipping in Iris Gray scrapbook.
37. James Quirk, *Photoplay*, June 1926, p. 101.
38. Dorothy Herzog, "Unique Motion Picture," *New York Mirror*, undated clipping in Iris Gray scrapbook.
39. Regina Cannon, "The Paramount School Graduates 16 Players," *New York Graphic*, undated clipping in Iris Gray scrapbook.
40. *Fascinating Youth* review, *Motion Picture*, June 1926 (clipping from Iris Gray's scrapbook).
41. *Fascinating Youth* review, *Motion Picture Classic*, May 1926 (clipping from Iris Gray's scrapbook). The quote from Dix was apparently meant to support the reviewer's contention. The implication was that there must be something intrinsically wrong with an institution that would have weeded out a star of Dix's stature.
42. *Fascinating Youth* review, *Variety* ("Fred"), 17 March 1926, p. 39.
43. One of Claud Buchanan's stage credits before joining the school had been in Anderson's revue *Jack and Jill*, which had featured Ann Pennington.
44. "Paramount Pupils in Publix Show," *Exhibitors Trade Review*, 9 April 1926, p. 1.
45. "Movie Actresses Visit Police Headquarters," *Boston Globe*, 20 May 1926.
46. Unidentified Kansas City clipping, Iris Gray scrapbook.
47. According to financial records preserved in the *Fascinating Youth* script file, the picture had a negative cost of $322,000, and reported domestic earnings of $268,000 and foreign earnings of $115,000 (AMPAS).
48. "Exceptional Find in Iris Gray From Paramount Acting School," *Exhibitors Trade Review*, 27 March 1926, p. 7.
49. "Paramount Sets Date for Second School Session," *Exhibitors Trade Review*, 23 July 1926, p. 1.
50. "Paramount to Drop School for Acting," *Exhibitors Trade Review*, 29 October 1926, p. 1.
51. Charles Paton, "School is Dismissed," *Motion Picture Classic*, June 1927, p. 70.
52. Ibid.
53. Paramount pressbook for *Rolled Stockings*. Sam Gill points out that the title *Sheiks and Shebas* had already been copyrighted by another company for a series of shorts.
54. "'Fascinating Youth' Brings Box-Office Publicity Dynamite!," *The Close-Up*, 8 May 1926, p. 3.
55. "Paramount Sets Date for Second School Session," *Exhibitors Trade Review*, 23 July 1926, p. 1.
56. "Paramount to Drop School for Acting," *Exhibitors Trade Review*, 29 October 1926, p. 1.
57. "Sixteen Lucky Students," *New York Times*, 18 October 1925, IX:5:6.

58. See Roi A. Uselton, "The Wampas Baby Stars," p. 88.
59. "Shrewsbury's Season Opens," *New York Times*, 9 July 1935, 24:4; "Show Finally Goes On," *New York Times*, 11 July 1935, 24:3; "Farce-Comedy at Deal," *New York Times*, 23 July 1935, 24:3.
60. See Luther Hathcock, "Whatever Happened to Cowboy Star Jack Luden?"
61. Kevin Brownlow, "William Beaudine," in Karr (ed.), *The American Film Heritage*, pp. 94–95.
62. This particular quote is from "Exceptional Find in Iris Gray From Paramount Acting School," *Exhibitors Trade Review*, 27 March 1926, p. 7.
63. Unidentified clipping, Iris Gray scrapbook.
64. *Los Angeles Times*, 23 January 1930 (clipping from USC Special Collections). Since First National was even then preparing its film *Show Girl in Hollywood*, the fact that anyone was moved to select "the most beautiful show girl in Hollywood," and that the title went to a First National contractee, seems a bit suspicious. Still, Jeanne *was* selected over all the rest at the studio. By the time of this story, incidentally, she was spelling her first name simply as "Jean." Interestingly, this article gives a brief outline of Jeanne's background, undoubtedly compiled from information supplied by Jeanne herself, but makes no mention whatever of Paramount or the school.
65. See Gregory Mank, "Marian Marsh Recalls Filming Svengali with Barrymore." This article, based primarily on an extended interview with the actress, never mentions her older sister.
66. Paramount Pictures School graduation program, 2 March 1926.
67. *Fascinating Youth* review, Variety ("Fred"), 17 March 1926, p. 39; *Fascinating Youth* review, *New York Times* (Mordaunt Hall), 10 May 1926, 19:1.
68. Charles Paton, "School is Dismissed," *Motion Picture Classic*, June 1927, p. 70.
69. Jesse L. Lasky, *I Blow My Own Horn*, p. 194.

Fascinating Youth

Famous Players-Lasky/Paramount, 1926
Copyright © 23 August 1926 by Famous Players-Lasky Corp. (LP23043)
7 reels (6882 ft)

Director: Sam Wood
Scenario: Paul Schofield, based on a story by Byron Morgan
Camera: Leo Tover
CAST: Charles Rogers (Teddy Ward)   Ralph Lewis (John Ward)
Ivy Harris (Jeanne King)   Joseph Burke (Ward's secretary)
Jack Luden (Ross Page)   James Bradbury, Sr. (the Professor)
Walter Goss (Randy Furness)   Harry Sweet (the Sheriff)
Claud Buchanan (Bobby Stearns)   William Black (deputy sheriff)
Mona Palma (Dotty Sinclair)
Thelma Todd (Lorraine Lane)
Josephine Dunn (Loris Lane)
Thelda Kenvin (Betty Kent)
Jeanne Morgan (Mae Oliver)
Dorothy Nourse (Mary Arnold)
Irving Hartley (Johnnie)
Gregory Blackton (Frederick Maine)
Robert Andrews ("Duke" Slade)
Charles Brokaw (Gregory)
Iris Gray (Sally Lee)

Themselves:
   Richard Dix   Chester Conklin
   Adolphe Menjou   Thomas Meighan
   Clara Bow   Lila Lee
   Lois Wilson   Lewis Milestone
   Percy Marmont   Malcolm St. Clair

Public Opinion and the Waite Murder Case

First published: *Griffithiana* 55/56 (Settembre 1996), pp. 64–71 (including separate Italian translation). Reprinted by permission.

Another Blanche Sweet article. By 1996 a number of things had changed since my Unpardonable Sin *piece was published; among other things, I had become a regular attendee of Le Giornate del Cinema Muto in Pordenone, Italy, and had happily accepted an invitation to the editorial board of their journal* Griffithiana. *In the meantime I was still pursuing my Blanche Sweet research. Since 1996 marked Blanche's centenary year, the Giornate mounted a special program of her films—including* Public Opinion, *which had only just been restored by the wizards at the U.S. Library of Congress. This article was published as a companion piece to that showing. Here again I've turned up a smattering of new research material in the meantime, and have fine-tuned the text accordingly, but this is essentially the same article that was published in 1996.*

Thank you: Madeline Matz and Michael Mashon (Library of Congress), Kristine Krueger (Academy of Motion Picture Arts and Sciences), Russell Merritt, Piera Patat, Livio Jacob, Annette D'Agostino Lloyd, and David Gerstein.

PUBLIC OPINION AND THE WAITE MURDER CASE

The silent cinema is an endless source of fascinating discoveries, and as research continues into the career of Blanche Sweet, more and more such discoveries are coming to light. Some of them lead in unexpected and surprising directions.

The plot of *Public Opinion* (Lasky/Paramount, 1916) revolves around a murder trial, and in reviewing the trade press coverage, one finds a couple of casual references to an actual murder case. "The big court room scene," says a press release, "is an exact replica of that in which the trial was held upon which the story is based."[1] This comment might easily be discounted, for Lasky publicity was forever making such claims. But another reference turns up in the *New York Dramatic Mirror* review: "While the story of 'Public Opinion' may not be based upon a recent New York murder case, the resemblance is apparent."[2] Upon investigation I found that there was indeed a resemblance, to a murder case far more sensational than the one depicted in the film.

The scenario of *Public Opinion* was the work of Lasky staff writer Margaret Turnbull. To show the power of public opinion to sway the workings of the criminal justice system, she devised a story of a nurse, wrongly accused of murder, who was "convicted" by gossip and yellow journalism before her actual court trial had even begun. This story was initially rejected by Lasky's director general Cecil B. DeMille, but the Lasky writing staff was so hard pressed to supply enough stories for the company's voracious production schedule that, early in 1916, company president Jesse Lasky authorized production of the scenario anyway.[3] It remained for Turnbull to augment her basic plot with enough colorful detail to make it an entertaining feature film.

She found her inspiration in a case which was currently in the news in her former home, New York City. On 12 March 1916, John E. Peck, a millionaire drug manufacturer from Michigan, died suddenly while visiting his daughter and son-in-law in New York. The purpose of his visit was to comfort his daughter over the loss of her mother, who had also died suddenly, six weeks earlier during a visit to the same couple. This curious coincidence prompted Peck's son Percy to request an autopsy, and then to contact a New York medical examiner for a second opinion. The second examination confirmed the findings of the autopsy: Peck's body contained a lethal dose of arsenic.[4]

The story broke in New York newspapers on 23 March, and suspicion immediately fell on Peck's son-in-law, Dr. Arthur Warren Waite. Waite had married Clara Peck, heiress to half her parents' fortune, the previous September after a three-week courtship. Her father had visited the couple in New York soon after the wedding and had returned home seriously ill, even before the two fatal visits. By late March, when John Peck's autopsy was performed, the grief-stricken Clara was back in Michigan and was herself experiencing severe stomach pain.

These basic facts might have been damning enough, but more evidence quickly emerged. Waite was listed as a "Doctor" in city directories, but it was discovered that he had never practiced medicine—he had taken a few courses in dentistry, but had never put them to use—nor, in fact, did he seem to have an occupation of any kind. His maid told police that Waite had put "medicine" into Peck's soup two days before the latter's death; and that, when Peck refused the soup because it tasted awful, Waite had put more of the same "medicine" into Peck's tea. Waite himself was unavailable for comment on any of this at first; the detectives who went to arrest him found him in a drug-induced stupor so intense that he could not carry on a coherent conversation for several days.

When interrogation did become possible, an even more sensational story began to take shape. Dr. Waite proved to be a tabloid editor's dream: a smooth-talking con man who had charmed and flattered his way into society and had simply taken whatever he wanted. Almost everyone liked him, including John Peck up to the time of his death, and his sister Catherine Peck of New York, with whom Waite had become friendly and who had recently given him $40,000 to invest for her. He also had a mysterious woman companion, with whom he had registered at the Plaza Hotel as "Mr. and Mrs. A.W. Walters," along with numerous other hinted liaisons. For his part, Waite flatly denied any wrongdoing at first; then, when confronted with overwhelming evidence (including proof of his purchase of a large quantity of arsenic on 9 March), he calmly "confessed" to having bought the arsenic at the request of a suicidal John Peck. This story infuriated the Peck family, and Percy Peck voiced his belief that Waite had intended systematically to exterminate the whole family in order to acquire their fortune. (Later, Waite did confess that he had murdered his in-laws and had contemplated murdering his wife Clara, but even then he could not refrain from excuses. He blamed his misdeeds on a malevolent spirit, "the man from Egypt," who had exercised an evil influence over him. Clara in turn disputed this statement, claiming that Waite had never mentioned such a spirit to her.)

The press seized on this story with glee, and readers, fascinated by the sheer audacity of the suspect, eagerly followed the latest developments. Fresh outrages were revealed almost daily: books on poisons were found in Waite's apartment, some with bookmarks at significant passages; he had insisted on his mother-in-law's cremation (making an autopsy impossible) and on a hasty revision of his wife's will; after John Peck's death Waite had bribed the embalmer to testify that he had used arsenic in the embalming fluid. "Mrs. Walters," Waite's companion at the Plaza Hotel, was revealed to be Margaret Weaver Horton, a young singer who was married to a man twice her age. She and her husband told police that they believed Waite had intended to kill them too—but Mrs. Horton made several unsuccessful attempts to see Waite again, both in the hospital and later in prison. To give the story an added measure of intrigue, Percy Peck's request for an autopsy had been prompted not only by his suspicions but also by a mysterious warning telegram signed "K. Adams." For a time police suspected that the telegram had been the work of a blackmailer, but "K. Adams" eventually turned out to be Elizabeth Hardwick, a New Jersey schoolteacher who had had a chance meeting with Waite after the second murder and who was motivated only by her own suspicions.

Such a story seemed tailor-made for the movies; if anything, Margaret Turnbull's fictional villain was tame compared to Arthur Waite. In her story Blanche Sweet appeared as a young nurse, innocently involved with a doctor—until she discovered he was married, whereupon she promptly left him. Shortly afterward, hired as a nurse to an ailing older woman, she learned that her new patient was the wife of her former lover. When the woman died under suspicious circumstances, the police investigation brought to light Blanche's earlier affair with the doctor. Lurid press coverage of the crime quickly branded her as the guilty party. Just as in real life, a sensational case was "tried" in the press and in the minds of the public before it ever came to court—except that, in the Waite case, the maligned suspect was the doctor, and really was guilty! There was no real-life counterpart to Blanche Sweet's nurse character. In fact, during his mother-in-law's illness, Waite had actively discouraged the employment of a night nurse and had practically ordered the day nurse out of the house.

Blanche Sweet appeals to the jury in a courtroom scene in *Public Opinion*. Lasky publicity claimed that the courtroom set, designed by Wilfred Buckland, was modeled on the actual courtroom in which the Waite case had been tried. Courtesy Academy of Motion Picture Arts and Sciences.

And, to be sure, the film story contained other elements that had nothing to do with the real-life case—some of those elements possibly built into Margaret Turnbull's scenario *before* the shocking facts of the Waite case came to light. One notable device in the film was the reappearance of the murdered woman, in spirit form, visiting the courtroom during Blanche's trial to try to sway the opinions of the jury. These "ghost" scenes were at odds with the relatively realistic action in the rest of the film, and elicited mixed reactions from critics. Some reviewers felt the scenes were "handled with considerable dignity,"[5] while others opined "that the story would suffer none from the absence of this 'spirit stuff'."[6]

Still, the Waite case provided a wealth of topically colorful incident which could be worked into the *Public Opinion* scenario. The basic situation of a doctor marrying a rich woman, then poisoning her for her money, would have been enough to remind 1916 audiences (at least those in the New York area) of the Waite case. To this basic resemblance were added assorted details. The fictional doctor, played by Earle Foxe, was made a smooth, cunning womanizer like Dr. Waite. Clara Peck Waite had been persuaded by her husband to reduce the charitable contributions in her will and to divert the money to him instead; Foxe, in the film, is seen watching anxiously as his wife gives money to the poor. Her son's (Tom Forman's) distrust of the doctor is evident from the beginning, a screen parallel to the suspicions of Percy Peck. And Foxe is eventually undone by the machinations of a blackmailer (Raymond Hatton), suggesting the New York district attorney's original theory concerning the "K. Adams" telegram—while Hatton's drug habit, and Foxe's own apparent familiarity with drugs, recall Waite's heavy overdose when he was about to be apprehended.

As Margaret Turnbull was developing her scenario for the film, the original furor over the Waite case peaked and then began to subside. Coverage in the press dwindled to an occasional cursory item. But it surged back onto the front pages when Waite's actual trial began on 22 May, just about the time the film was going into production.[7] All the testimony in the case was reported in detail, but the trial lasted less than a week. By the time production of *Public Opinion* was complete, Dr. Waite had been found guilty of first-degree murder and had been sentenced to the electric chair.

Once the trial had ended, little more was heard of the Waite case. Dr. Waite's attorneys started a half-hearted appeal, but this attempt came to nothing. The case's impact was manifested in a new ruling by the New York Board of Health: henceforth a body could not be cremated without an investigation by the police department. Dr. Waite was left in the Tombs, and later in Sing Sing, to await execution. There he chatted amiably with reporters, composed poetry—some of which was reprinted in the papers—and, belatedly, turned to God. His serenity lapsed in late July when, with a sliver of broken glass, he slashed his chest. The warden of the death house at Sing Sing contemptuously dismissed this act, not as a serious suicide attempt, but as a mere bid for attention. "The scratch is infinitesimal," he assured the press. "It was not even serious enough for hospital treatment."[8] Thereafter Dr. Waite reverted to his former calm, and was forgotten by the press until he went to his death in May 1917. Even then he reportedly "smiled and hummed a tune" when informed of the scheduled date and time of his execution.[9]

In the meantime, in August 1916, *Public Opinion* was released by Paramount Pictures. It opened to generally good notices, although some reviewers found the plot far-fetched. "Like every good melodrama," wrote W. Stephen Bush in *Moving Picture World*, "this film play shrivels up under a logical analysis. There are improbabilities right on the surface and many more just a little below the surface."[10] Bush, like some other reviewers, was merely referring to the plot mechanics, which involved convenient coincidences. He might have added that, improbabilities notwithstanding, truth was far stranger—or, at any rate, *less* probable—than this particular fiction.

Notes

1. "Public Opinion," *Moving Picture World*, 26 August 1916, p. 1422.
2. Public Opinion review, *New York Dramatic Mirror*, 26 August 1916, p. 26.
3. These and many other matters are documented in a large selection of DeMille-Lasky correspondence (edited and annotated by James D'Arc) reproduced in *L'eredità DeMille/The DeMille Legacy*. For correspondence directly related to *Public Opinion*, see pp. 343, 355, and 369–70.
4. This account of the Waite case is a radically condensed digest of the story as reported in the *New York Times*, beginning 23 March 1916. The case was regularly featured on the *Times*' front page through the end of March, as scandalous new information surfaced daily. After the first of April the coverage subsided somewhat, but it returned to the spotlight late in May when the trial began, and lingered in the *Times*' pages well into the summer. Subsequently Dr. Waite earned one final flurry of headlines at the time of his execution in May 1917.
5. *Public Opinion* review, *New York Dramatic Mirror*, 26 August 1916, p. 26.
6. *Public Opinion* review, *Motography* (George W. Graves), 2 September 1916, p. 558.
7. Surviving records from the Lasky studio are sparse, and do not indicate exact production dates for films of this period. They do indicate that the original scenario of *Public Opinion* was purchased from Margaret Turnbull on 24 January 1916, before Dr. Waite had committed either of his murders. They also show that the negative was completed 12 June 1916, while that of *The Dupe*, Blanche Sweet's previous Lasky feature, was completed 8 May 1916. A letter from Blanche Lasky to her brother, dated 30 May 1916 (*L'eredità DeMille*, p. 343), speaks of the development of the *Public Opinion* script in the past tense, and a May 1916 calendar can be seen in an office scene in the first reel. Cecil DeMille's letter to Lasky, expressing surprise at finding the story currently "in operation," is dated 6 June 1916 (*L'eredità DeMille*, p. 355). Combining all these facts, along with the striking resemblance of the film to real life, suggests that the company purchased Margaret Turnbull's original idea in January 1916; that it was then rejected for use by DeMille and others; that Lasky overruled the objection and Turnbull revised the scenario during the spring of 1916, while excitement over the Waite case was at its peak; and that actual shooting took place during late May and early June.
8. "Dr. Waite Slashes Chest," *New York Times*, 26 July 1916, 5:5.
9. "Waite Faces Chair Calmly," *New York Times*, 20 May 1917, 11:2.
10. *Public Opinion* review, *Moving Picture World* (W. Stephen Bush), 2 September 1916, p. 1532.

Public Opinion

Lasky production 143
Lasky/Paramount, 17 August 1916
Copyright © 29 July 1916 by Jesse L. Lasky Feature Play Co. (LP8834)
5 reels (4591 ft)

Director: Frank Reicher
Scenario: Margaret Turnbull
Art director: Wilfred Buckland
Camera: Dent Gilbert
CAST: Blanche Sweet (Hazel Gray)
             Earl Foxe (Dr. Henry Morgan)
             Edythe Chapman (Mrs. Carson-Morgan)
             Tom Forman (Phillip Carson)
             Elliott Dexter (Gordon Graham)
             Raymond Hatton (Smith)

"It Was Always Funny Working with Fields:" Producing *Sally of the Sawdust* and *That Royle Girl*

First published: *Griffithiana* 62/63 (Maggio 1998), pp. 38–79 (including separate Italian translation). Reprinted by permission.

This article came out of the confluence of three elements. One was my interest in Paramount Pictures as a comedy studio. In the 1990s I was struck by the fact that, of all the major studios (as distinct from smaller boutique studios like Hal Roach), Paramount was by far the most conducive to comedy during the 1920s and '30s. I still think it's not a coincidence that W.C. Fields, the Marx Brothers, and others made their best films at Paramount during those years. Another element was the Griffith Project at Pordenone, which was just ramping up in 1997, and in which I would be honored to participate over the next twelve years. In all the excitement over Griffith, I couldn't help noticing the serendipity: two films, directed by D.W. Griffith, starring W.C. Fields, and produced at Paramount!

Finally, of course, there were the Sintzenich diaries themselves, which provided a unique opening for researching those two films. I am forever indebted to the indispensable Madeline Matz, then at the Library of Congress, whose countless services to countless historians over the years included facilitating my access to those diaries.

I'm particularly pleased to have the opportunity to revisit this article, and to correct a mistake that has embarrassed me ever since 1998. After the article was already in print, Richard Koszarski pointed out that I had incorrectly claimed that Barnet Bravermann was a second eyewitness to production of the two films. I won't make excuses; this was just simply wrong—Bravermann was not in Griffith's orbit during the 1920s and didn't conduct his Griffith research until years after the fact. My thanks to Richard for pointing this out, and my apologies to Piera and Livio for committing this mistake in their fine journal.

And now, at last, I have a second chance to publish the article as it should have been! This is gratifying because, apart from that mistake, the truth is that I took some pride in this piece. Tracking the production of the films, day by day, gives us a unique historical perspective on them. When Griffithiana *was issued at the 1998 Giornate with this article in it, John Stone, a regular festival attendee, suggested a second article along the same lines. He pointed out that Griffith's great postwar drama* Isn't Life Wonderful, *filmed partly on location in Europe and similarly documented by Sintzenich, was ripe for this day-by-day treatment. I think it was a great idea, and it may well be a future project.*

Thank you: Madeline Matz and Richard Franklin; Richard Koszarski (American Museum of the Moving Image) and Howard Prouty (Special Collections, Margaret Herrick Library, Academy of Motion Picture Arts and Sciences); Nancy Kauffman (George Eastman Museum); the motion picture staffs of the Library of Congress and the Museum of Modern Art; Russell Merritt, Mike Gebert, John Bengtson, and Annette D'Agostino Lloyd; and Piera Patat and Livio Jacob.

"IT WAS ALWAYS FUNNY WORKING WITH FIELDS"

PRODUCING *SALLY OF THE SAWDUST* AND *THAT ROYLE GIRL*

Considering the profusion of classic films that emerged from the mid-1920s, it's hardly surprising that *Sally of the Sawdust* and *That Royle Girl* (both 1925) tend to be overlooked today. Both were regarded as relatively minor efforts, and *That Royle Girl*, generally acknowledged as the lesser of the two, is at this writing considered a lost film. Yet both films are worthy of note, if only for one reason. They represent a unique collaboration between two legendary, if seemingly mismatched, cinematic talents: D.W. Griffith and W.C. Fields.[1]

The making of *Sally of the Sawdust* and *That Royle Girl* marked a turning point in Griffith's career, and not an altogether pleasant one. For the first time in more than ten years, he was reduced to the status of a contract director. Enormous prestige was still associated with Griffith's name, and he was nominally the head of his own company, but he was assailed by financial problems which had become impossible to ignore. Accordingly, in 1924 he contracted with Famous Players-Lasky to direct three features, the first two of which became the films under discussion here. In return Famous Players was to shore up his ailing financial condition. Both Griffith and Famous Players put the best possible face on the situation, the latter proudly hailing Griffith as a distinguished addition to their stable of directors, which he surely was. But this professional downgrading sounded an ominous note for the great director's future.

From W.C. Fields' perspective, conversely, these films represented a golden opportunity. Through two decades of hard work Fields had established himself as a popular favorite on the vaudeville and legitimate stage, but, despite a few cursory screen appearances, success in the movies still eluded him. The stage musical *Poppy* proved an ideal transitional medium, for it provided Fields not only with a highly visible vehicle, but with a character. Eustace McGargle, the garishly costumed, cheerfully outrageous circus huckster, was a role tailor-made for Fields' talents, and crystallized his image with the theatre-going public. When *Poppy* was filmed as *Sally of the Sawdust* it ushered Fields into the movies with a ready-made persona, one which endured for the remainder of his career and is still fondly remembered today.

As it happens, we have been granted a privileged look at the making of these two films. Hal Sintzenich, a cameraman who had worked with Griffith on several films (including his most recent, *Isn't Life Wonderful*), was with him again for these two features. This gives us the incalculable benefit of an eyewitness account: Sintzenich's diaries, which he maintained throughout these years and whose faithful daily entries recorded countless details of production. Today this priceless resource is preserved in the Library of Congress.[2] It's supplemented by another, included in the D.W. Griffith Papers collection at the Museum of Modern Art: the notes of Griffith's would-be biographer, Barnet Bravermann. Among the typed transcripts of Bravermann's interviews with former Griffith associates, his handwritten daily notes on Sintzenich's career are an anomaly—sometimes quoting verbatim from the diaries, sometimes offering unique insights and perspectives that *also* seem to come directly from the former cameraman. We might speculate that Bravermann reviewed the diaries in Sintzenich's company, sometimes transcribing the entries, sometimes recording Sintzenich's observations in hindsight.

Whatever the case, these two sources, taken together, provide a richly detailed account. As the two films take shape day by day, many facets of Griffith's working method are revealed. Given his circumstances, one might have pictured him as a broken, discouraged man; instead we see him plunging into the filmmaking process with undiminished zest. As a seasoned professional, Griffith demonstrates his ability to plan and shoot efficiently—and yet, on occasion, indulges his old penchant for spontaneous improvisation. Working in Famous Players' studio in Astoria, Long Island for the first time, he freely avails himself of that facility's resources. These include a choice of varied locations elsewhere on Long Island, many of which appear in *Sally of the Sawdust*, and the close proximity of the New York theatre district and its vast pool of talent. Not least among those talents is Fields himself, who is headlining the *Ziegfeld Follies* at night while he works in Griffith's films by day. Here, too, we see Fields blossoming as a screen performer, contributing his own material from the beginning—material developed during a long, self-supervised apprenticeship in show business, and carefully nurtured for such an opportunity as this.

The following is a chronology of the making of *Sally of the Sawdust* and *That Royle Girl*. It is based primarily on the Sintzenich and Bravermann accounts, fleshed out with additional information derived from correspondence and contracts in the Griffith Papers, along with material from trade publications, New York and Chicago newspapers, the Paramount script files, and other sources. Direct quotes from Sintzenich and Bravermann will be self-evident; other references are separately annotated.

Monday, 3 September 1923: Dorothy Donnelly's musical comedy *Poppy* opens on Broadway at the Apollo Theatre, featuring Madge Kennedy in the title role and W.C. Fields as Professor Eustace McGargle. (For the record, the cast also includes Robert Woolsey, five years before his teaming with Bert Wheeler.) Both Fields and the show are highly successful, and *Poppy* continues for a long run.

Tuesday, 10 June 1924: D.W. Griffith, experiencing severe financial difficulties, enters into a contract with Famous Players-Lasky, the producing arm of Paramount Pictures. The contract calls for Griffith to direct three films for Famous Players, while the latter agrees to procure a $250,000 loan for Griffith's company.

December 1924: The first chapter of Edwin Balmer's "That Royle Girl" appears in *Hearst's International* magazine. The story concerns a free-spirited Chicago girl named Joan Daisy Royle; her idol, a popular jazz bandleader, who is framed for the shooting of his estranged wife; and the stern, upright Assistant State's Attorney who prosecutes the case and with whom Joan Daisy eventually falls in love. A supporting character in the story is Joan Daisy's roguish, charming stepfather, known in Balmer's original as "Dads." Chapters continue to appear on a monthly basis (switching over to another Hearst publication, *Cosmopolitan*, after three chapters) through the following July. Later in 1925 the story is published in book form by Dodd, Mead and Company to generally favorable reviews.

1925

Saturday, 10 January: Despite his pending contract with Famous Players-Lasky, Griffith contracts to direct yet another film for United Artists.

January–March: Famous Players-Lasky acquires the screen rights to *Poppy* (the Paramount script files do not indicate the precise date) for $15,000. This story is designated as the first of Griffith's three films for the company. He later claims that he suggested it himself, and that it was the only one of his three films for the company (the other two being *That Royle Girl* and *The Sorrows of Satan*) that he really wanted to direct.[3] For the time being, the film retains its working title *Poppy*.

During the following weeks, Griffith assembles his cast and crew. Despite W.C. Fields' success in the stage version of *Poppy*, he is not automatically given the role of McGargle in the film. Bravermann's notes include the observation that Fields and Famous Players had haggled extensively over terms: "It was a toss-up whether he was going to work for Paramount."

The camera crew is the subject of more negotiation; Griffith wants to use cinematographers who have worked with him in the past, while Famous Players-Lasky prefers its own contractees. The result is a compromise, one Griffith cameraman and one Famous Players cameraman working side by side. In the finished film, screen credit will be given only to FP-L's Harry Fischbeck and Griffith's Hal Sintzenich, but the film also includes shots filmed by Frank Diem (Griffith) and J. Roy Hunt (FP-L), among others. Diem has formerly worked as Griffith's still photographer.

Friday, 6 March: After waiting until nearly the last minute—shooting is set to begin the following Monday—the company finally signs Sintzenich, who reluctantly accepts a pay cut from his salary on *Isn't Life Wonderful*.

Monday, 9 March: The first day of shooting on the picture. The morning is devoted to lighting tests and rehearsals. In the afternoon the first scenes in the story become the first scenes photographed: a prologue in which Poppy's [Sally's] mother is turned out of her home for marrying a circus man.

Tuesday, 10 March: The company begins by finishing the scenes from the day before, with Effie Shannon and Erville Alderson, and proceeds to the bedroom set to film the scene in which Shannon finds her daughter's childhood possessions. By 3 p.m. this scene is also finished; the next scenes scheduled are those in Carol Dempster's tent, but the tent set is not yet ready.

Wednesday, 11 March: This day marks the filming of Fields' first scene in the picture: another prologue scene in which he enters Poppy's mother's tent to find the latter on her deathbed, and subsequently adopts the child. This scene is completed during the morning so that Fields can be at the New Amsterdam Theatre in time for a *Ziegfeld Follies* matinee. During

W.C. Fields, as the colorful circus huckster, fleeces the locals in D.W. Griffith's *Sally of the Sawdust.* Courtesy George Eastman Museum.

the afternoon J. Roy Hunt, a Paramount cameraman normally assigned to Bebe Daniels, helps the camera crew set lights for the interior of the great circus tent, a process that lasts all afternoon and evening. It is nearly midnight by the time the crew finishes and leaves.

Thursday, 12 March: Having prepared the giant circus tent the night before, the company shoots the crowd scenes in and around it. Two hundred extras are hired for the day, so the morning's output consists mostly of long shots, featuring crowds of spectators and also the circus performers and animals, returning to the main tent after the parade. During the afternoon the spectators are filmed entering the tent, then assembled around the various sideshows.

Friday, 13 March: Smaller-scale circus scenes are filmed, beginning with a lion tamer who feeds the lion pieces of meat from his own mouth. (The film's publicity will identify the lion as Jim, a veteran movie performer whose credits include Kathlyn Williams serials, "Tarzan" films, and the Goldwyn Pictures trademark.[4]) Then the company moves to the trapeze set for the scenes featuring Carol Dempster, in her first scenes to be filmed, and Glenn Anders. In the afternoon the "ballyhoo" scenes, featuring Fields and Dempster with a group of spectators, are begun. This is where Fields first performs his famous juggling act for the camera, this time using tennis balls.

Fields is not the only member of the cast who is concurrently appearing on the New York stage. Glenn Anders, who first appears as the lecherous acrobat on this day, is simultaneously playing a leading role in Sidney Howard's *They Knew What They Wanted* at the Klaw Theatre. And of course Alfred Lunt, who will play the romantic lead in this film, is appearing opposite Lynn Fontanne in *The Guardsman*.

Saturday, 14 March: Completion of the "ballyhoo" scenes. The day begins with closeups of Carol Dempster, followed by her act with Fields. Again, care is taken to complete Fields' scenes for the day during the morning hours, to accommodate his matinee appearance. In the afternoon, closeups of Dempster and Anders are made on the trapeze set, to be cut into the scenes filmed the day before. These are followed by more miscellaneous shots of the sideshows, ending with shots of Dempster with Lucy, the elephant.

Sunday, 15 March: This first weekend of production sets the pattern for the ebb and flow of Griffith's work: when production is in full swing, Griffith works long hours—including Saturdays and Sundays—and expects his company to do the same. This long day's work is devoted to scenes featuring Fields, principally the fight scene and the shell game ("the old army game"). These scenes also feature Tammany Young, a longtime Fields crony who will appear in many of the comedian's later films.

Monday, 16 March: Most of the day's shooting takes place on the set of Carol Dempster's tent. The major scenes filmed during the day are those of Anders' attack on Dempster and of Fields' intervention, smashing Anders over the head with a breakaway bottle.

Tuesday, 17 March: Having filmed the medium shots of the attack scene in Dempster's tent on the previous day, Griffith films the closeups for the same scene. The company then moves back to the great circus tent and shoots more parade scenes, and finally scenes of the stranded circus. By day's end, the company has finished with both sets.

On this day Sintzenich and Diem are informed that Roy Hunt will be working with them for three weeks until the next Bebe Daniels picture starts shooting. Diem is strongly opposed to Hunt's presence and threatens to quit. Sintzenich is more sanguine; although he recognizes that it means a loss of prestige for himself, "I think it will get Mr. Griffith away from his old fashioned ideas of lighting."

Wednesday, 18 March: After a morning off, Sintzenich spends the afternoon with an electrician, going over the lighting for the next day's shooting on the interior of the bootleggers' house.

Thursday, 19 March: The first day's shooting on the bootleggers' set. Diem, still upset and allegedly sick, does not report for work; Hunt is scheduled but has worked all night with the Daniels company; so Sintzenich is the only cameraman on the set. Viewing the rushes the next day, he decides he has used too many lights.

Friday, 20 March: In the morning the closeups are filmed for the bootleggers' scene; the company is finished with the set by lunchtime. The scenes of Fields inside the bakery oven are filmed in the afternoon. This is Hunt's first day on the *Poppy* set, and Griffith gives him a free hand.

Saturday, 21 March: Back to the cutaway oven set, for the shots in which Carol Dempster (absent on the previous day of shooting) unwittingly raises the heat on Fields inside the oven. The afternoon is devoted to arranging the lights on the main bakery set, and on the large set of Judge Foster's home, for use during the next few days.

Sunday, 22 March: The remaining bakery scenes are filmed on the main bakery set, with Fields, Dempster, and two extras. This darkly comic sequence will depict Fields nearly cooked inside the oven; Sintzenich comments that "The episode, I think, will be very funny when cut."

Monday, 23 March: Work begins on the set of Judge Foster's (Erville Alderson's) home. After rehearsing all morning, the company starts shooting in the afternoon. First to be filmed are all the entrances and exits in the set, filmed as a group (another characteristic of Griffith's method), then the medium shots and closeups. Griffith, like many of his company, is suffering from a severe cold and leaves for his doctor's office at the end of the day. Frank Diem finally returns to work on this day.

Tuesday, 24 March: Griffith, still sick, does not appear at the studio until 3 p.m. The company passes the time in rehearsal, concentrating on Carol Dempster's and Effie Shannon's scenes together, and shoots a test of the

Foster set as lighted for the society ball. On this night Griffith elects to screen the rushes, not at the studio, but at a facility which will often be used for this purpose in succeeding months: Miles Projection Rooms in Manhattan. (If the company had stayed at the main studio long enough to see the rushes, Bravermann observes, Griffith would have had to pay them overtime.)

Wednesday, 25 March: The company starts shooting the society ball and entertainment in the Foster home. Over 100 extras are hired for the day, so this day's work is dominated by crowd scenes of the dance. Dempster's tableaux and specialty dance are also begun.

Thursday, 26 March: Shooting of the ball continues, retaining some of the extras. The day's output features more Dempster tableau scenes, and her scenes with Effie Shannon and guests. This day marks Alfred Lunt's first appearance on the set.

Friday, 27 March: More scenes in the Foster home. The day's work begins with night scenes in the hall set with Dempster, Lunt, and a dozen extra men, then resumes in the large set with Dempster and Shannon at the piano, interrupted by Alderson. The day concludes with closeups of Roy Applegate as the detective.

Saturday, 28 March: The company returns to the Foster hall set for the entire morning and most of the afternoon, then makes retakes and inserts of Dempster in the bakery and tableau sets. At the end of the afternoon's shooting, plans are made for lighting of the big carnival set.

Sunday, 29 March: Most of the day is devoted to a dinner scene, which is rehearsed in the morning and filmed in the afternoon. Afterward the company returns to the Foster hall set and films the arrival of the guests, including Fields, Dempster, and Lunt.

Monday, 30 March: Dempster's costume changes are filmed on the boudoir set. Diem and Sintzenich film these scenes on the studio's basement stage while Hunt is on the main stage, lighting the carnival set.[5] On finishing the boudoir scene, the company sets up on the carnival set and makes some tests. Fields' absence (he is "flirting with pneumonia" and has missed several *Follies* performances) prevents them from proceeding further.

Tuesday, 31 March: The company starts work on the carnival set, beginning with closeups of Dempster and Lunt on the carousel and the interruption of their love scene by Charles Hammond, as Lunt's father. The meeting of Dempster and Lunt with the children is also filmed, and the day's work ends with a shot of the carousel itself.

Wednesday, 1 April: In the morning the company films a scene at the back of Fields' tent, with Anders trying to convince Dempster to stay with the circus. (A comment appears at this point in Bravermann's notes that Griffith "never acted for them - he explained the situation & relied on their feeling.") In the afternoon Hunt shoots some retakes of Dempster's closeups, and the day ends with two short scenes of dancing acts.

Thursday, 2 April: Griffith films crowd scenes at the Green Meadow carnival, with 250 extras. The crew works steadily until 7 p.m., filming a total of 11,000 feet of crowd scenes between four cameras. Harry Fischbeck, a Paramount cameraman who has arrived the previous day from the West Coast, observes the day's activities but does not photograph.

Friday, 3 April: Fischbeck officially joins the *Poppy* camera crew. The company is still on the carnival set, this time shooting the "daylight" scenes of preparations for the carnival opening—long and medium shots and closeups. Griffith is so intent on the sequence that he continues to work nonstop; when he finally calls "Lunch" at 2 p.m., a roar goes up from the assembled crowd of electricians and prop men. In the afternoon Fields' carnival act (including more juggling) is filmed, finishing about 7 p.m.

Saturday, 4 April: Apart from some miscellaneous closeups, the day is devoted to rehearsals of the main carnival scenes, to be started the next day.

Sunday, 5 April: A long day which produces over 10,000 feet of raw footage, mainly closeups on the carnival set, featuring all the principals and about 25 extras.

Tuesday, 7 April: After shooting an insert of the sign over the carnival entrance, the company spends the morning on comedy scenes with Fields. Sintzenich notes that Fields performed both "his fiddle & newspaper gag" and "the flirtation & fly paper gag." He considers the latter by far the funnier of the two, and Bravermann's notes include the observation that Fields kept the crew laughing constantly during his rehearsals. In the afternoon and evening the company shoots exteriors of the tent, including its collapse.

Wednesday, 8 April: The morning is again given over to Fields, in particular his three-card monte and shell game scenes, and his subsequent arrest and escape. Back to the tent exterior in the afternoon, for scenes of the aftermath of the tent's collapse. These include Dempster's attempted escape by crawling under the edge of the tent, and her arrest.

Thursday, 9 April: The scenes outside Fields' tent, in which Dempster tells him about her meeting with Lunt at the carousel, are filmed. In the afternoon Fields' getaway is retaken, followed by a scene with Anders and one of the circus women. (Bravermann: Griffith "had a lot of circus people in picture.") The courtroom set being ready, the afternoon concludes with rehearsals there.

Friday, 10 April: Shooting on the courtroom set begins with long shots, featuring most of the principals and 30 extras playing spectators. The action includes Dempster's attempted escape. These scenes are followed by closeup reaction shots of some of the principals. The usual nightly screening of rushes is a discouraging experience this time, owing to the poor quality of the prints.

Saturday, 11 April: More closeups in the courtroom set, mainly those of Erville Alderson and Carol Dempster. Sintzenich puts gauze over the lens for two shots of Dempster, then asks Griffith if he would like one shot without the gauze and reports that "he jumped down my throat for using it." Sintzenich explains to his diary, if not to Griffith, that Fischbeck uses excessive lighting for closeups and had expressly asked him (Sintzenich) to use the gauze for these shots. As far as possible the company works around Fields, who is unavailable on this day because of a matinee.

Sunday, 12 April: More courtroom scenes, this time featuring Fields. The entire finish of the courtroom sequence, from Fields' dramatic entrance through the reunion of Dempster, Shannon, and Lunt (followed by Fields' inconspicuous exit), is filmed this afternoon, after which the cast and crew pose for publicity stills. Griffith, still unhappy with the print quality of his rushes, sends one reel of negative to his laboratory at Mamaroneck as an experiment.

The film's title evidently has not been changed at this point; Sintzenich refers to Dempster's character as "Poppy" in his notes for the day.

Monday, 13 April: The morning is spent on the courtroom set making inserts of Dempster, the afternoon on the basement stage filming long shots of the prison scenes. Some of the previous days' rushes, including the reel processed at Mamaroneck, are found acceptable, but the remainder are so disappointing that it looks as if all of Sunday's work will have to be redone. Griffith, speculating that a new and unfamiliar cameraman may have something to do with the problem, leaves instructions for Fischbeck to look at certain reels the next morning.

Tuesday, 14 April: While Fischbeck screens the offending rushes, Sintzenich has his assistant unload and clean all his magazines, as he (Sintzenich) has been noticing scratches in his own shots. The company assembles on the courtroom set to reshoot Fields' entrance and his reunion with Dempster, then returns to the prison set and films Dempster's closeups in her cell and in the warden's office. This evening the rushes are satisfactory.

Thursday, 16 April: The company shoots miscellaneous inserts and retakes in the prison set and Alderson's office set, and is finished by noon.

Friday, 17 April: Location shots for the film commence on this day when a small party, consisting of Erville Alderson, Glenn Anders, and the camera crew, travels to the Long Island town of Syosset. Alderson is cast as Judge Foster in this film—and has earlier appeared on both stage and screen, for Griffith and others—but also functions as a Griffith assistant. He handles some minor administrative functions for the company and, on this occasion, even directs some incidental scenes while Griffith is occupied elsewhere. These scenes depict Anders' arrival at, and departure from, a small-town railroad station. The Syosset station is used for this purpose; the company makes shots of both the noon and 4 p.m. trains. (Fischbeck shoots the first alone, since the truck bearing some of Sintzenich's equipment does not arrive until after the noon train's departure.) Over the next six weeks, Griffith will utilize numerous scenic locations around Long Island, New York, and Connecticut as exteriors for the picture.

Monday, 20 April: Famous Players-Lasky buys the screen rights to Edwin Balmer's still-unfinished novel *That Royle Girl* for $35,000, more than twice the amount paid for *Poppy*. Subsequently the company circulates the story among some of its contract directors—all of whom, including Griffith, promptly reject it.

Wednesday, 22 April: The bulk of production being finished for the current picture, Diem and Sintzenich receive layoff notices. Sintzenich goes to say goodbye to Griffith, who tells him the layoff is only temporary.

Monday, 27 April: Griffith invites some of the cast and crew to Miles Projection Rooms to view a rough cut of the picture, without exteriors.

Sunday, 3 May: Griffith, pleased with the Syosset railroad station shots, takes the company back for more, this time featuring Carol Dempster and W.C. Fields. The two are photographed in the station, performing the sandwich scene, and walking down the tracks. Sintzenich, back on the payroll, is part of the camera crew, but a child on the station platform knocks over his camera and damages the iris attachment. Sintzenich patches it up as best he can, but due to various delays it will not be replaced until three weeks later.

Monday, 4 May: More location shots, this time in Greenwich, Connecticut, using the palatial estate which has been selected to represent the Fosters' home. Many of the principals are filmed outside the house, as are some guests arriving for the ball. The Hatch family, owners of the house, are on hand all day to watch the filming. Most of the day's usable shots are made in the morning, as the sky clouds up in the afternoon.

Tuesday, 5 May: A long day devoted to more railroad shots. Griffith, having engaged a special train at the Long Island City station, takes it to Hicksville where Fields and Dempster are filmed arriving on foot and jumping a passing train. The company's locomotive breaks down here, so another is procured. Setting up the cameras on a flatcar immediately behind the engine, the crew films Fields and Dempster climbing aboard a car, sitting in the open doorway, and being washed off the train by the water spout. A comment quoted in Bravermann's notes: "Griffith enjoyed these scenes."

Wednesday, 6 May: Back to Greenwich, for exteriors of a house known as "The Castle" which has been selected to represent Alfred Lunt's home in the picture. Miscellaneous shots are taken, including a long shot of Lunt leaving the house. At the entrance, the scene of Lunt's meeting with Dempster as she helps the fallen child is retaken. The Hatch family, owners of the house used two days earlier, invite the company to lunch with them in the garden.

Friday, 8 May: Griffith and Alderson having spent the previous day scouting locations, the company goes to Flushing and spends a long day in Kissena Park, filming chase scenes with Dempster and a gang of extras.

Saturday, 9 May: The company goes to Huntington, where the Town Hall has been selected to represent the exterior of the courthouse. Long shots of the building's imposing façade are followed by shots made in the rear, as Dempster escapes through a high window and climbs down a tree. This action is filmed several times, with Dempster herself and with a stunt double named Miss Case.

Sunday, 10 May: An attempt is made to shoot exteriors of the bootleggers' house, represented by a house in Douglastown. Fields is filmed entering and exiting the house, and in some chase scenes, but rain interferes with shooting for most of the day.

Tuesday, 12 May: The weather having improved, the rest of the Douglastown exteriors are filmed. These include more scenes of the house, Fields' theft of the flivver and subsequent getaway, and the diversionary scene with the oxen.

Wednesday, 13 May: The company sets up at the Long Island Speedway in Islip and spends the entire day filming Fields being chased by the bootleggers, and vice versa.

Thursday, 14 May: More chase scenes, this time filmed in Rosyln. (Perhaps in the spirit of the scenes, some of the company are stopped for speeding on their way to the location. On learning their identity, the policeman lets them go.) Tracking shots are made in the morning, with Fields' car preceded by a camera car which contains an Akeley and Sintzenich's Pathé. Stunt scenes are made in the afternoon, with Fields' car crashing through fences and overturning in a field. For these scenes, Fields is doubled by a stunt driver named Loomis.

Friday, 15 May: Fields' scene at the crossroads and his argument with the cop are filmed in the morning. So is the episode in which Fields, struck from behind by water from a gardening hose, assumes that a small puppy nearby is responsible. Sintzenich later confirms that such bits of business in the film, as in his stage acts, were contributed by Fields himself. Bravermann quotes him: "Scenario? Doubt it. If so, it read 'Fields ad lib.' Fields invented most of the funny episodes. It was always funny working with Fields."

In the afternoon more Fields/bootlegger chase scenes are made along the Long Island Motor Parkway, including some stunt skids performed by Loomis. Sintzenich notes that the company is still shooting at 8 p.m., "the latest yet."

Saturday, 16 May: Two locations are utilized today: Flushing, for the bakery exteriors, and Bayside, for a sequence in which Dempster is frightened off the porch of a house. Sintzenich: "It was late when we finished although we did very little shooting."

Sunday, 17 May: Returning to Bayside, Griffith makes miscellaneous shots of all the principals. The company is joined by James ("Gentleman Jim") Corbett and his wife, who distribute cold ale to the group, and later is given a tour of the Talmadge home. The day concludes in Russell Gardens, a Great Neck housing development, with shooting of the closing scenes of the picture which show Fields established in a new "army game": selling real estate!

Monday, 18 May: Having decided that he needs more exteriors of Lunt's home, Griffith takes the company back to Greenwich for more shooting at "The Castle." Lunt is filmed walking on the terrace, and leaving and arriving at the house "in a beautiful new Rolls Royce." In the afternoon a Fields/Dempster scene is filmed in town, followed by the cemetery scenes with Dempster and Lunt, and a scenic shot of a farmhouse.

Tuesday, 19 May: Back to the studio for a day of miscellaneous large closeups of Dempster, wearing various costumes, against various backgrounds.

Wednesday, 20 May: Closeups of Dempster and Lunt are filmed on a grass plot at the studio, to be cut into the cemetery scenes filmed in Greenwich two days earlier. These are followed by closeups of Alderson, after which some of Dempster's prison and conservatory scenes are remade.

Thursday, 21 May: By now the bulk of shooting is finished, and only odds and ends (and retakes) remain to be done. This morning inserts of Dempster and Alderson are made for the courtroom scene, and Dempster's closeups for the bakery scene are remade. In the afternoon the company returns to Bayside to retake Fields' real estate scenes.

Friday, 22 May: Studio inserts are made showing Dempster and Fields on the railroad car, to match with the shots taken on location. In the afternoon, more inserts: Dempster and Fields in the gambling tent, and Applegate in the courtroom.

Wednesday, 27 May: Taking advantage of an appearance by Sparks Circus in Jackson Heights, Griffith takes his company there for circus atmosphere shots. Pitching of the big tent and preparations for the performance are filmed, as is the parade. The circus performers, honored to be hosting Griffith's company, invite them to lunch in the mess tent. Afterward Fischbeck and Sintzenich set up inside the main tent and film the major acts. Sintzenich is impressed with the authenticity of these shots; Bravermann later writes: "the two cameras being in *the audience—a real audience at a real show.*" All in all, about 4,000 feet of genuine circus material are filmed on this day.

May–July: By now production of *Sally of the Sawdust* (as the picture has been renamed) is essentially complete. Sintzenich films inserts of letters and telegrams on 29 May, and 1 June sees a location trip to Whitestone for exteriors of yet another railroad station, the "Whitestone" sign covered by one reading "Green Meadow." For the most part, however, Griffith is preoccupied with editing and titling the film. Occasionally he decides that further inserts (usually closeups of Carol Dempster) are needed, and the camera crew dutifully supplies them—one such shot being made as late as 10 July, after production has already started on the next film. On 12 June Griffith requests an insert for the shell-game scene, showing Fields' hands performing his trickery. Fields is not summoned to the studio for so minor a shot; the hands in the closeup are those of actor Charles Slattery.

Sintzenich, still on the payroll, hangs around the studio but has little to do; one day he is assigned to go on location to Great Neck to shoot some scenes for Bebe Daniels' next picture, *Wild, Wild Susan*.

On 19 June Famous Players and United Artists enter into a contract which acknowledges that *Sally of the Sawdust* has been produced by the former company, but allows for it to be released by the latter, according to the terms of the January contract. Gross receipts are to be divided between the two companies according to a specified schedule, the greater percentage going to Famous Players. Griffith thus satisfies two contractual obligations with a single film.

As *Sally of the Sawdust* begins to assume its final form, Griffith tries it out in numerous previews. Notable among these is a four-day run in Patchogue, 21–24 June. United Artists executives also view the picture on 16 June and offer their own suggestions, usually for cuts. The general consensus: Fields' scene with the bootleggers and subsequent chase, Dempster's pursuit by the police, and the courtroom scenes are too long and should be cut. Adolph Zukor sees the film on 30 June and, though he professes great admiration for it, echoes these suggestions. During this time

Louis Silvers is working on the musical score, constantly revising it to keep pace with revisions in the picture.

Meanwhile Griffith is readying his next production. Sintzenich mentions on 20 June that Griffith is rehearsing "his new story" and that he has rejected *That Royle Girl*. Within two weeks, however, *That Royle Girl* has become the next Griffith picture, with Carol Dempster again in the title role.

Monday, 6 July: The first day of shooting on *That Royle Girl* begins with scenes featuring a Griffith veteran, James Kirkwood, as the District Attorney, and Ida Waterman as his mother, on the set representing Kirkwood's family home. The rest of the day is devoted to tests of Carol Dempster and other members of the cast.

Tuesday, 7 July: On the same set, Griffith shoots a telephoning sequence and scenes of a dance. At the end of the afternoon, all of Kirkwood's entrances and exits in the hall set are photographed.

Wednesday, 8 July: Famous Players-Lasky hosts a luncheon for journalists, in honor of Griffith's first film under his new contract. (This of course is the *second* film under his contract, but the first to be released as a Paramount picture.) Luncheon is served on the set, and the guests meet some of the cast and are addressed briefly by Griffith. Then, under the impression that this is the first day of production, they watch as he begins rehearsals. Sintzenich reports only that "Mr. Griffith spent practically the whole day rehearsing one scene & finally had to change one of the actors," but does not elaborate on the scene or the players in question. In the evening, Sintzenich shoots more tests of Carol Dempster in various costumes and headdresses.

Thursday, 9 July: In a day of intense activity, the company sets up on Marie Chambers' apartment set and films the murder sequence.

Friday, 10 July: On Harrison Ford's apartment set, Griffith shoots a sequence of Ford (as the bandleader) and his wife, along with accompanying scenes of hallway traffic. At the end of the afternoon, yet another closeup of Carol Dempster is filmed for *Sally of the Sawdust*—ten days before its Chicago opening.

Saturday, 11 July: The company moves to Kirkwood's office set and shoots all the scenes there in one day. Viewing the rushes two days later, Sintzenich considers them "punk."

Monday, 13 July: Back on Ford's apartment set, Griffith shoots the scene in which Ford shows Dempster around the apartment and plays the piano for her. In the evening Griffith screens two earlier Paramount pictures, *Cappy Ricks* (1921) and *Manhandled* (1924), before starting the rushes— perhaps for the purpose of evaluating players for the role of Dempster's father, which has not yet been cast.

Tuesday, 14 July: Griffith rehearses, then shoots, the arrival of the detectives, their questioning of Dempster and Ford, and Kirkwood's interview with the suspects.

Wednesday, 15 July: The company films closeups and inserts of the questioning scenes, to cut into the material filmed the previous day. After this, all the entrances and exits in Ford's hallway set are filmed. The evening screening of rushes at Miles is preceded by a studio screening of six reels of sample print of *Sally of the Sawdust* for the upcoming Chicago opening.

Thursday, 16 July: After finishing the inserts started the day before, Griffith shoots tests of two possible candidates for the role of Dempster's father. The possibility of using W.C. Fields in the role is not even mentioned at this point. Instead Griffith tests another popular comedian from the New York stage: Ed Wynn. Later in the day Erville Alderson is also tested. Wynn's test is evidently unsatisfactory, and Alderson is tentatively cast in the role. Alderson is, in any case, better suited to the author's original conception of the character as a courtly, charming fraud than is Wynn. Subsequently Wynn does star in a Paramount comedy, *Rubber Heels* (1927), but the bulk of his career will be divided between media in which his voice can be exploited: stage, radio and television, and sound films.

This day's work finishes with more costume tests of Dempster. The evening's rushes are of more than usual interest; Sintzenich feels that his closeups of Dempster, taken the previous day, "were the finest & most beautiful it has been my good fortune to photograph." He notes that Griffith and Dempster also seem quite pleased with them.

Friday, 17 July: On the eve of the company's departure for Chicago to open one picture, Griffith is still feverishly working on the next. Today he begins work on Dempster's home set, shooting numerous scenes featuring Dempster, Kirkwood, Ford, and the detectives. The evening sees more screening of *Sally* sample prints.

22 July 1925: D.W. Griffith, seated at left, takes advantage of a personal-appearance junket to shoot scenes of Carol Dempster, right, against authentic Chicago backgrounds for *That Royle Girl*. Hal Sintzenich, who did so much to document the making of these films, is at Griffith's side, cranking the Pathé camera. Courtesy George Eastman Museum.

Saturday, 18 July: During the morning, Griffith manages to finish more shots in the same set—closeups of Dempster, and a medium shot of her argument with the detectives—before leaving for Chicago. This trip serves a dual function: it allows Griffith and some of his principals to attend the Chicago opening of *Sally of the Sawdust*, and it offers the opportunity for location shots of the city. Author Edwin Balmer has not only set *That Royle Girl* in Chicago but has made the city an integral part of his story, and though Griffith and his writers have taken generous liberties with the plot, this aspect of the original is retained. Consequently Griffith is accompanied on his journey by a large group of cast and crew members.

Sunday, 19 July: Arriving in Chicago in the afternoon, Griffith and his assistants and cast members put up at the Blackstone Hotel, while members of the crew check in at the more economical Auditorium. Throughout the ensuing week Griffith displays his skill at public relations, often pausing to converse at length with local journalists. Early in the week he tells one reporter that "the spirit of Chicago" is "something I can't define. It's in the very atmosphere, if I could only catch it."[6] Toward the end of his stay, however, he tells the same reporter that "I think we have caught it," going on to comment expansively on the people of Chicago.[7]

Monday, 20 July: *Sally of the Sawdust* opens at the Roosevelt Theatre in Chicago. The first showing, at 9:35 a.m., plays to a packed house. In the afternoon Griffith's camera crew goes to the Wilson Avenue district and films panoramic shots of the street, filled with bathers, and of the beach. Setting up at another beach, at the Drake Hotel, they make one shot before being stopped by the police. The entire party attends the 7:30 performance of *Sally*. Griffith addresses the audience from the stage and, amid thunderous applause, introduces Kirkwood, Ford, and finally Carol Dempster. (Fields, still headlining the *Follies* in New York, is not along for this trip, but sends Griffith a congratulatory telegram.) The picture is judged a great success, winning rave reviews from Chicago critics. Emerging from the theater, Griffith is introduced to local society girl Mary Meeker and promptly offers her a small part in his new film—an enterprising act which earns him considerable extra space in the local press.

Tuesday, 21 July: With the Chicago run of *Sally* safely launched, Griffith's party tackles the making of location shots in earnest. On this day the entire company returns to the Wilson district, where Carol Dempster is filmed walking along various streets with one of Griffith's assistants, and inside a drugstore where she plays a scene at the soda fountain with Ford. In the afternoon more local-color scenes are filmed at the beach. The company is surrounded by crowds, who make working conditions difficult but who are good-natured and eager to watch a movie being made. Mary Meeker gets her promised movie exposure, appearing in both the street and beach scenes, and later confides to Dempster that the experience was "lots of fun."[8] Griffith also picks out other bathers from the throng and uses them in establishing shots.

Wednesday, 22 July: In Lincoln Park, Dempster is filmed visiting the memorial statue and communing with the spirit of Lincoln. (The Lincoln statue is mentioned once in Balmer's story, but not in connection with the title character; the idea that the girl idolizes Lincoln is strictly a Griffith invention.) Later Dempster is photographed alighting from a bus, and again the company is surrounded by spectators whom Griffith again uses to advantage. Other scenes for the day feature Dempster walking with Kirkwood in a park (and, once, with the city and Lake Michigan in the background) and entrances and exits at a well-known local dance hall.

Thursday, 23 July: In the morning, establishing shots are made at Cook County Jail, including entrances and exits by Kirkwood. Once again Griffith cannily includes one of the locals—Paul Gilbert, a reporter on the *Chicago Evening Post*—in the scene. After filming exteriors Griffith tours the jail, the courtrooms, and the State's Attorney's offices, taking notes for later use in studio set design (although Kirkwood's office scenes have already been shot!). Early in the afternoon the entire company boards the Century Limited for the return to New York. Except for an incident in which the train plows into a car stalled at a crossing (no one is hurt), the trip is uneventful.

Friday, 24 July: Arriving at Grand Central Station late in the morning, the company goes directly to the studio and back to work. Setting up on the Dempster home set, Griffith shoots scenes with Dempster, Erville Alderson (provisionally cast as Dempster's father), and an actor named Dewey. This may be the Arthur Dewey who had appeared as George Washington in Griffith's *America*.

Saturday, 25 July: After shooting miscellaneous entrances and exits on the Dempster hallway set, Griffith returns to the main apartment set and films a sequence with Dempster and Frank Allworth as a newspaper reporter. In the evening some of the group watch the scenes shot in Chicago. Sintzenich: "They were only fair, nothing to write home about."

Monday, 27 July: After a rare day off, the company assembles on the set of the dressmaking establishment. Griffith spends the morning in rehearsal, then makes scenes in the afternoon with a number of extras cast as models and with another New York stage comedian, Bobby Watson, as Hofer, the proprietor of the establishment. Watson impresses onlookers, including Sintzenich, with his cleverness. For the duration of the silent period he will alternate between occasional stage and screen appearances, but with the coming of sound he will find steady work in the movies as a character player.
    In the evening, instead of rushes, Griffith screens a new print of *Sally*, this time for the New York opening.

Tuesday, 28 July: Back on the dressmakers' set, Griffith films the scenes in which Dempster begins as a presser and is promoted to become a model. (None of this is in Balmer's original story.) Some tension is developing between the cameramen; Sintzenich comments that "it is useless to make any suggestions to Fischbeck, as he seems to resent it."

Wednesday, 29 July: On the hotel room set, Griffith films the scenes in which Kirkwood detains Dempster and Ford for questioning. These are followed by rehearsal and shooting of unspecified scenes with Dore Davidson and Bobby Watson.

Thursday, 30 July: A few more shots are made on the hotel room set. On this day, more than three weeks after the start of production, W.C. Fields tests for the role of Dempster's father. His tests are satisfactory but he and Famous Players are unable to agree on terms. By the end of the day, the talk around the studio is that Fields will not be in the picture and that Alderson will continue in the role. (Two days later, however, Fields does begin work in the picture.) This day's work ends with rehearsals on the main stage in the courtroom set. The evening screening of rushes is delayed because Griffith is scheduled to speak on the radio.

Friday, 31 July: Rehearsals continue on the courtroom set all morning and into the afternoon. In mid-afternoon Griffith begins to shoot the scene of Ford's indictment. In the evening he screens another special print of *Sally* for the New York opening.

Saturday, 1 August: Back to the dressmakers' set. Featured in the day's scenes are a group of extras as models, Kirkwood, Dempster (as a model), Bobby Watson, Ida Waterman, Alice Laidley—and W.C. Fields, who has apparently resolved his financial disagreement with Famous Players and is making his first scenes in the picture as Dempster's father.

Sunday, 2 August: The New York opening of *Sally of the Sawdust* at the Strand Theatre. Mordaunt Hall of the *Times* offers a fair assessment: "Mr. Griffith's last production, 'Isn't Life Wonderful?' was an artistic success, but it failed in many towns to attract the crowds. In 'Sally of the Sawdust' Mr. Griffith only nods to art but bows low to the box office."[9] But Hall's general reaction to *Sally* is positive, and other critics are downright ecstatic. Some of them lavish warm praise on Carol Dempster's performance, and there is unanimous agreement that the screen has found an outstanding new comedian in W.C. Fields.

Monday, 3 August: Galvanized by the *Sally* reviews, Griffith plunges back into the shooting of the *Royle Girl* courtroom scenes. One hundred extras are hired for the day, so most of the day's work consists of long and medium shots. Fischbeck and Sintzenich, between them, expose over 10,000 feet of film. Later, looking at the rushes of the dressmakers' scenes filmed on Saturday, Sintzenich feels that "they were awful & looked like a lot of junk. Any second assistant at the studio could do better."

Tuesday, 4 August: On the courtroom set again, but without the extras, Griffith shoots closeups of Kirkwood, Dempster, and Ford. Miscellaneous shots are made with some of the witnesses, but Fields' scenes are postponed as he is not present.

Wednesday, 5 August: On the courtroom set for yet another day, Griffith works mainly with Fields and Watson, and once again is obliged to finish with Fields' scenes by 1:30 so that the latter can play a matinee. In the afternoon, more courtroom scenes are filmed with Ford, Dempster, and Kirkwood. Ending the afternoon with some scenes in the entrance hallway, the company finishes with the courtroom set.

Thursday, 6 August: After a conference over lighting the next big set, the cabaret, the company spends the morning on the hotel room set with Dempster, Fields, Kirkwood, and Watson. In the afternoon, on the dressmakers' set, Fields is filmed getting a free lunch and then being thrown out by Watson.

Friday, 7 August: The first day on the cabaret set, this time with 175 extras. Aside from comedy scenes featuring Fields and Dewey (the latter made up with a long beard), most of the day's work involves dance scenes. The specialty dancers include a group from *George White's Scandals*, headed by Alice Weaver, who creates a sensation in the studio. Sintzenich reports that "Bill Steiner, one of the camera assistants, was picked out by Mr. Griffith to do the Charleston, & he did it admirably."

According to the film's publicity, Dorothea Love, credited in the cast list as "Lola Neeson" ("Nesson" in the original story), one of Ford's more ardent admirers, is also picked out of the crowd of extras by Griffith while working on this set.[10] Unfortunately her career in featured parts seems to begin and end with *That Royle Girl*.

Saturday, 8 August: Work continues on the cabaret set. In the morning the scene with Fields joining his daughter's party is started, but cannot be finished because of the sudden illness of Dewey, who is appearing in the scene. Work on other, unspecified cabaret scenes continues in the afternoon.

Sunday, 9 August: Having fallen behind in screening rushes during the previous week, Griffith's company convenes at the studio to screen some 30 reels. The scenes are considered generally quite satisfactory.

Monday, 10 August: Back on the cabaret set in the morning, Griffith finishes the Fields/Dewey scenes which had been interrupted on Saturday. In the afternoon he returns to the set of Dempster's apartment. All the scenes which had been filmed there with Alderson appearing as her father must now be retaken with Fields in the role.

Tuesday, 11 August: More retakes on the Dempster apartment set, substituting Fields for Alderson. Finishing these in the late afternoon, Griffith begins rehearsing on the set of the Boar's Head Inn, a roadhouse which serves as headquarters for a group of gangsters involved in the killing of the bandleader's wife.

Wednesday, 12 August: A day of location shooting. First, at an apartment house in Flushing, all the principals are filmed in miscellaneous entrances and exits. In the afternoon the company moves to Jackson Heights, where a house has been selected to represent Kirkwood's home. He is filmed leaving the house in his car and, in a couple of shots, speeding along the road.

Thursday, 13 August: Griffith spends the morning inspecting the exterior "hurricane set," which is being prepared for shooting. Balmer's original story climaxes with a car chase by gangsters; Griffith later declares that "since no one could find an ending that seemed to mean anything, we worked out the idea of putting in a storm or cyclone."[11] This invention is tacked onto the story and becomes the film's major setpiece, adding considerably to the budget but providing an appropriately spectacular Griffith climax. Most of the film's reviews will refer to the storm as a "cyclone," but Sintzenich invariably refers to the exterior set as "the hurricane set."[12] The afternoon is spent in further rehearsals in the Boar's Head Inn interior. No scenes are photographed, save a couple of Dempster costume tests. In one of her gowns, reports Sintzenich, she looks "perfectly stunning."

Friday, 14 August: A long hot day in the studio, shooting on the Boar's Head Inn set. The scene is one in which Dempster tries to get information from Paul Everton, cast as the gang leader. Griffith is suffering from a cold but works steadily through the day. Fischbeck and Sintzenich are informed on this day that their assistants—Arthur De Titta and Joe Low, respectively—are being promoted to first cameramen, and that they will be getting new assistants. Low is made an Akeley specialist, and De Titta will later work on Griffith's *The Sorrows of Satan*.

Saturday, 15 August: More work on the set of the Boar's Head Inn, beginning with inserts for the scenes filmed the previous day, and ending with scenes of panic as the storm begins.

Monday, 17 August: The action moves to the upstairs hallway set of the Boar's Head Inn, where chase and fight scenes are filmed. After working on these all day, Griffith and his crew spend the evening on the hurricane set, laying out the camera positions and making some tests. Griffith's "wind machines" are a dozen airplane propellers furnished by the Curtiss company, many still mounted on fuselages.

Tuesday, 18 August: After working late the night before, the company gets a late start and films only a few interior shots of Dempster's escape from Everton's gang at the Boar's Head Inn.

Wednesday, 19 August: Work continues on Dempster's escape scenes, started the day before. Griffith demonstrates his long-standing fondness for improvising on the scenario, in this case building up a scene for one of the gangsters, making of him "a 'gorilla' type of gunman as per Lon Chaney."

Thursday, 20 August: Griffith shoots his first scenes on the hurricane set, beginning in mid-afternoon and lasting well into the night. No scenes of the actual storm are filmed in this session; the set is the exterior of the Boar's Head Inn, and the first shots are those of guests arriving and departing in their cars. These are followed by the scene of Dempster's escape from an upstairs window, moving hand over hand along a suspended ladder to another building. As in *Sally of the Sawdust*, she is doubled in these shots by Miss Case.

Friday, 21 August: A day of scheduled location work is cancelled because of rain. Back at the studio, Griffith shoots interiors of the Inn, with Dempster and Frank Allworth overhearing Everton's self-incriminating words in the next room. Some hallway scenes are also retaken.

Saturday, 22 August: Work begins in earnest on the hurricane set. The company will continue on this set for the next week, usually working at night. This night Griffith shoots scenes of the beginning of the storm, including Dempster's attempted escape and recapture by the gang. This is followed by closeups of Dempster on the ladder and roof of the lean-to, and finally by the collapse of the barber shop upon which she is standing. (All the buildings on the hurricane set are breakaway buildings, designed for repeated destruction or collapse as needed.)

Sunday, 23 August: More shots of Dempster's escape and recapture, followed by some dangerous storm action: the falling of a telegraph pole, a tree, and a small house. Sintzenich: "So far we have had good weather & it has been fairly warm."

Monday, 24 August: Griffith begins by retaking part of the escape/recapture scene. This time Dempster is doubled by Miss Case for the shots in which she is nearly hit by falling objects, including the telegraph pole. Bravermann's notes mention that this scene was further intensified afterward by lightning (created by scratching a frame of the film) and rain. Griffith also shoots closeups of some of the gang members.

All this is merely a prelude to the main business of the evening: This is the night on which the main storm action is to be shot. The principal event here is the collapse of the Boar's Head Inn exterior, a spectacle which must be repeated three times because the building refuses to come down all at once. Because of the expense and the spectacular nature of this scene, extra camera operators are recruited for the night. Altogether there are fifteen cameras working, including at least two Akeleys. None of these added cameramen are credited onscreen, but Sintzenich identifies some of them: George Peters, William Miller, and Charles Gilson.[13]

Tuesday, 25 August: Having filmed the peak of the storm action the night before, the company begins filming rescue and comedy-relief scenes. Kirkwood's arrival at the Boar's Head Inn and his frantic search for Dempster, buried under the rubble of the building, are filmed first. Next Fields' stunt double is filmed being blown through the scene on a pushcart. Finally Griffith shoots scenes of the rescue party, locating and digging for Dempster and the gang under piles of debris.

Wednesday, 26 August: As the storm continues to subside, the company films scenes of relief workers arriving. Sintzenich writes admiringly of one Griffith improvisation: relief workers of many nationalities and ethnic backgrounds are shown uniting in their humanitarian efforts, giving away supplies to the homeless and refusing payment. Finally, closeups of Kirkwood, Dempster, and Allworth are shot for inclusion in the rescue scene.

Thursday, 27 August: More Fields comedy scenes are filmed in the afternoon. These include his entrance carrying a goose, his fight with a taxi driver, and the beginning of his ride in the pushcart. Later Griffith films more hurricane action: Miss Case, doubling for Dempster, crouches by a bush and is narrowly missed by the side of a house blowing through the scene.

Friday, 28 August: The company's last night on the hurricane set is devoted to scenes of the aftermath: Kirkwood driving through in his car, his way blocked by falling trees, and more traffic scenes featuring the taxi and Fields' pushcart. The night's work ends with closeups of Kirkwood. Some of the crew drive home in the Packard used in the picture as Kirkwood's car.

Saturday, 29 August: Back to the studio. The call is for 3 p.m., but Sintzenich arrives two hours early to clean the sand and dirt—souvenirs of a week in front of the wind machines—out of his camera. The day's work consists of miscellaneous pickup shots of Everton and members of his gang, including scenes which further build up the gangster's "gorilla" character. Extensive rushes of the previous week's work are viewed during the afternoon; everyone, including Griffith, is quite pleased with them.

Sunday, 30 August: Back on a daytime shooting schedule, the company commutes to Douglastown for location shots. These show Fields being blown into a lake with a coop of geese, the coop surfacing with only the heads of the geese visible, and Fields eventually blown ashore. Griffith uses four of the Curtiss wind machines and lavishes much effort on these scenes, but the consensus is that they are disappointing; Fields, rather than "doing his stuff" in the water, merely looks frightened.

Monday, 31 August: Back in the studio, Griffith shoots more interiors of the Boar's Head Inn. These depict Dempster's discovery of the real killer's identity and her fight with Florence Auer, cast as the gang leader's girlfriend.

Tuesday, 1 September: Completion of the scenes started the previous day. After making numerous closeups of Dempster and Auer and remaking some of the medium shots, Griffith finishes with shots of the gang breaking down the door with an axe.

Wednesday, 2 September: The Dempster apartment set having been reconstructed, Griffith shoots the closing scenes of the picture with Dempster, Kirkwood, and Fields. Like *Sally of the Sawdust*, this film is crafted on such a grand scale that Griffith is using sets on both of the Astoria studio's levels of stages. Sintzenich eloquently describes the atmosphere: "The studio is like a mad house with so many companies working. There is D W. Griffith, Gloria Swanson, Adolph [sic] Menjou, Tommy Meighan, Richard Dix, Monte [sic] Bell & Brenon all working at the same time, seven companies going full blast, jazz bands, brass bands, symphony all trying to outdo each other, & the carpenters & props drowning the lot."

Thursday, 3 September: The company films scenes of Everton and his gang in his office and florist's shop. Once again Griffith builds up character by improvising business; in this case Everton's personality is embellished with a scene in which he gently toys with a white rose while issuing instructions to his murderous gang. The final scene of the day is a retake of a Dempster/Kirkwood love scene on the couch.

Friday, 4 September: On the Dempster "first home" set, Griffith films a scene in which Fields brings in a group of bums to play checkers, and another scene in which Dempster announces that she has quit one job and taken another. While rehearsing in the morning, the company receives a visit from Gloria Swanson and a group of her titled English guests. Later Kirkwood is filmed in a stationary car before a rotating "panorama" background, giving the impression of a rapid tracking shot, as he rushes to Dempster's assistance during the storm. The long day concludes on the basement stage, where a scene with Dempster and a landlord is filmed.

Saturday, 5 September: The company continues to work methodically through the remaining scenes. Today the manhandling of Dempster and Allworth in the cellar set is committed to film. Unhappy with the amount of dust thrown into the scene, Griffith exchanges heated words with Alderson, who leaves the set and is not mentioned again in Sintzenich's diary. The day's final scenes are those of a ceiling cave-in "which looked great," according to Sintzenich.

Sunday, 6 September: This is not a scheduled shooting day, but Griffith is behind schedule and anxious to finish the picture, and so issues a call for noon. The company works on the prison set, shooting Ford's entrance after being sentenced, several scenes in his cell, and a condemned prisoner being led past Ford's cell to the gallows. (The next day being Labor Day, the company *is* given the day off.)

Tuesday, 8 September: After retaking some of the courtroom shots to include a group of flappers among the spectators, Griffith returns to the prison set, having just received a telegram from T. A. Brockmeyer of Cook County Jail. Griffith has evidently requested details of uniforms and practices used there; armed with this information, he finishes the prison scenes with Ford and Dempster. Ford's release from prison is also filmed, with the flappers from the courtroom scene waiting to greet him. Finally Griffith, unsatisfied with the ceiling cave-in scenes, tries another take.

Wednesday, 9 September: Work begins on the last major set of the picture, a cabaret called King Tut's Tavern. "It was a splendid piece of work," writes Sintzenich, "& the detail & paint work very pleasing." As with previous large sets, the first day's work involves a crowd of extras—two hundred, in this case—and consists mostly of long shots. Dempster's entrance with Allworth is filmed, as are long shots of her solo dance.

Thursday, 10 September: Work continues on the cabaret set, for scenes representing two different parts of the story. The first of these is a New Year's party; in the second Everton, Auer, and Sally Crute are joined at their table by Dempster, who is wearing a wig and disguised as a French dancing girl. Sintzenich is impressed with her disguise. Still later, closeups of her entrance and her solo dance are made.

Friday, 11 September: A location trip to film exteriors at the 92nd Street Ferry on Long Island. Working in a "hot, dirty smelly & stuffy street" and surrounded by a crowd of ragged youngsters, Griffith films scenes of Dempster's family's eviction from their tenement, including their fight with the landlord and landlady. Despite the unpleasant working conditions, the consensus is that these scenes are very funny.

Saturday, 12 September: Working in the studio tank, Griffith shoots closeups and retakes of Fields' adventures in the water with the geese.

Sunday, 13 September: More tank shots of Fields and the geese. Bravermann, after echoing Sintzenich's disappointment in Fields' work in the Douglastown location shots, adds the comment here that "He did his stuff better in the studio."

14–22 September: By now most of the production work is finished, and Griffith is either away on business or occupied with cutting the picture. In any case, Sintzenich is not on hand to report on studio activities during most of this time, as he is confined to bed with a severe case of "grippe" for about a week. (His condition is probably not helped by having attended an all-night bachelor party for his former assistant, Joe Low, on the 14th.)

Wednesday, 23 September: Still unsatisfied with Fields' scene with the geese, Griffith shoots more material for it in the glass tank at the Hippodrome. *Exhibitor's Trade Review* reports that "Griffith moved in with lights and cast following the evening performance."[14]

24 September–2 October: Sintzenich, recovered, returns on the 24th to "a very different looking studio" with only two companies at work. Griffith's company (having worked late at the Hippodrome the night before) is not one of them, and for the next week, while Griffith is absorbed in the editing room, Sintzenich hangs around the studio with nothing to do. To pass the time he shoots a few inserts for Monta Bell's *The King on Main Street*.

Saturday, 3 October: Griffith, in the throes of cutting *That Royle Girl*, starts filming the odd scenes he needs to fill in. This day is scheduled for exteriors, but because of rain the company stays at the studio while Fischbeck and Sintzenich shoot miscellaneous inserts of Dempster in her various costumes.

Tuesday, 6 October: The weather having cleared up, Griffith goes outdoors to film one of the earliest scenes in the picture: Dempster's fight scene with a newsboy, precipitating her firing from her newsstand job. Griffith's "location" is the newsstand at the Washington Avenue subway station, only a few blocks away from the studio. In the afternoon he films more inserts of Dempster, one of them a retake of a shot made the previous Saturday.

8–20 October: As production winds down, Sintzenich has only a few odd inserts to shoot. These include miscellaneous items of jewelry, Marie Chambers' hand holding a $2000 check, and simulated Chicago newspapers with specially printed headlines. The last shots made for the picture are still more closeups and inserts of Carol Dempster, photographed by Sintzenich and by two more uncredited cameramen: J. Roy Hunt and George Webber.

During most of this time, Griffith is still preoccupied with cutting the picture. On 15 October, Albert Grey writes him a long letter ("Realizing that you anticipate taking about 5,000 feet out of 'That Royle Girl' ... "), detailing his suggestions for cuts.

Meanwhile, on 13 October, the copyright in *Sally of the Sawdust* is transferred from D.W. Griffith, Inc. (Griffith's division of United Artists) back to Famous Players-Lasky. This is considerably ahead of schedule, the original agreement having called for *Sally* to remain United Artists' property for five years.

After more cutting, previews, and adjustments for censorship, *That Royle Girl* opened in late 1925. Modern writers sometimes suggest that the film was an unmitigated disaster, but in fact it received a number of enthusiastic reviews. (Paramount even considered a remake in 1932, an idea which generated a treatment called *Girl of Today* before being abandoned.) Today, tantalized by Griffith's handling of a strictly contemporary subject, the Fields connection, and the historical value of authentic Chicago location footage, one longs for another chance to see the film. It is true, however, that neither *That Royle Girl* nor Griffith's third Famous Players production, *The Sorrows of Satan*, proved the commercial success for which both he and the company were hoping. Whatever these films may have done for Griffith's artistic reputation, they did nothing to improve his commercial standing.

That Royle Girl marked the end of Hal Sintzenich's association with Griffith. His subsequent photographic adventures took him to several continents and culminated in a 20-year stint with the Pan American Institute of Geography and History. All this and more was faithfully documented in his diaries, which he continued to maintain well into the 1970s.

W.C. Fields, after his triumphant breakthrough in *Sally of the Sawdust*, suffered a disappointing reception in *That Royle Girl*. Critics recognized all too plainly that his inflated screen time was gratuitous; *Variety* reported that "He has nothing to do, and does it just like a man with nothing to do would do it."[15] Even so, Fields' exposure in the two Griffith films served as an auspicious introduction to movie stardom. "I have been looking forward to this," he told a reporter. "You know, for years they wouldn't even consider me for pictures. Now I can take my choice! And I'm quite ready. I have a number of ideas. I have several scenarios tucked away—wrote 'em myself—many 'gags' that have never been used, an idea for sub-titles that I don't believe has been used."[16] Fields was, in fact, so eager to launch his movie career that he withdrew prematurely from the *Ziegfeld Follies* in October 1925 to sign a contract with Famous Players. After a confrontation between Florenz Ziegfeld and Famous Players, Fields returned to the *Follies* until his contract expired in January 1926. With that, his movie career began in earnest. His connection with Paramount Pictures continued, off and on, over the next twelve years, and produced such fondly remembered comedies as *Running Wild* (1927), *Million Dollar Legs* (1932), *It's a Gift* (1934)—and, in 1936, a remake of *Poppy* under its original title, directed by Eddie Sutherland and co-starring Rochelle Hudson.

Notes

1. Griffith, with his image as a stern Victorian moralist, and Fields, with his image as an alcoholic misanthrope, may at first glance seem a filmic odd couple indeed. But their seeming disparity was more apparent than real; William K. Everson pointed out what a wonderful film could have resulted from Griffith's and Fields' common interest in Dickens. See Everson, *The Art of W.C. Fields*, p. 40.
2. See Barnouw, "The Sintzenich Diaries."
3. Letter, D.W. Griffith to Adolph Zukor, 10 November 1926. (The Griffith Papers also include a draft of a similar letter, addressed only to "Gentlemen" and dated 28 October 1926.)
4. "Movie Work Mere Detail For Lion," *Sally of the Sawdust* pressbook.
5. Paramount's Astoria studio, a building with a fascinating history of its own, had been operating since 1920. Essentially a complete state-of-the-art production facility contained under a single roof, it was built around an enormous "main stage" measuring 120 x 218 feet, under a 50-foot ceiling, and ringed by three floors of offices, dressing rooms, and lab facilities and carpentry shops. There was also a "basement stage" covering the same area. To accommodate numerous production units simultaneously, each stage area was designed to encompass multiple sets at any given time. See Koszarski, *Hollywood on the Hudson*, pp. 28–29.
6. Paul T. Gilbert, "Griffith Unable to Grasp Unique Spirit of Chicago," *Chicago Evening Post*, 20 July 1925, p. 1.
7. "Griffith Shoots Court Scenes for Chicago Movie," *Chicago Evening Post*, 24 July 1925, p. 2.
8. "Mary Meeker In Movie Debut," *Chicago Herald and Examiner*, 22 July 1925.
9. *Sally of the Sawdust* review, *New York Times* (Mordaunt Hall), 3 August 1925, 10:2.
10. "Griffith Plays Santa Claus to Movie 'Extra'," *That Royle Girl* pressbook. The pressbook story claims that Dorothea Love had been an unsuccessful applicant to the Paramount Pictures School, an in-house training program for young players (see pp. 17–42 in this volume).
11. Letter, Griffith to Zukor, 10 November 1926.
12. At this writing the exact location of the "hurricane set" is still a matter of conjecture. It clearly was not built on the back lot; historian Richard Koszarski, an authority on the Astoria studio, has confirmed that a production shot of the "hurricane" camera crew was taken against a background other than the studio (see Koszarski, *The Astoria Studio*, p. 32). The location was evidently a public sports facility; Sintzenich speaks of "the Ball Park" on his first visit to the set, and the *Royle Girl* pressbook (which is, of course, more concerned with publicity than with accuracy) speaks of "a large football park" near the studio. The context of Sintzenich's remarks confirms that this large exterior set was no great distance from the studio. To date, however, the combined efforts of several specialized film scholars have failed to pinpoint with certainty the exact location of the set.
13. Peters and Miller are referred to in Sintzenich's diary only by their last names. It's possible, of course, that "Miller" refers to Arthur Miller or Ernest Miller, but William

("Bill") Miller was a friend whom Sintzenich saw socially on occasion. He had also photographed several Paramount films at Astoria (most recently *The Shock Punch*) before being laid off in June. In contrast, neither Arthur nor Ernest seems to have had any Paramount ties at this point; this makes William easily the leading candidate.

14. "Production Highlights," *Exhibitor's Trade Review*, 3 October 1925, p. 47.
15. *That Royle Girl* review, *Variety* ("Sisk"), 13 January 1926, p. 40.
16. "W.C. Fields: 'Follies' Comedian Contemplates the Open Spaces of the Movies," *Boston Herald*, 4 October 1925.

Sally of the Sawdust

Griffith/United Artists, 2 August 1925
Copyright © 8 September 1925 by D.W. Griffith Inc. (LP21804)
10 reels (9500 ft)

Director: D.W. Griffith
Scenario: Dorothy Donnelly and Forrest Halsey, based on the play *Poppy* by Owen King and Dorothy Donnelly
Art director: Charles M. Kirk
Camera: Harry Fischbeck, Hal Sintzenich, and (uncredited) Frank Diem and J. Roy Hunt
Film editor: James Smith
Assistant directors: Erville Anderson, Frank Walsh
CAST: Carol Dempster (Sally)
W.C. Fields (Prof. Eustace McGargle)
Alfred Lunt (Peyton Lennox)
Erville Alderson (Judge Henry L. Foster)
Effie Shannon (Mrs. Foster)
Charles Hammond (Lennox Sr.)
Roy Applegate (detective)
Florence Fair (Miss Vinton)
Marie Shotwell (society lady)
Glenn Anders (Leon)
Tammany Young
Jim, the lion

That Royle Girl

Famous Players-Lasky/Paramount, 7 December 1925
Copyright © 8 December 1925 by Famous Players Lasky Corp. (LP22094)
10–11 reels (10,253 ft)

Director: D.W. Griffith
Scenario: Paul Schofield, based on the short story by Edwin Balmer
Art director: Charles M. Kirk
Camera: Hal Sintzenich and (uncredited) Harry Fischbeck, Joe Low, Arthur De Titta, George Peters, Bill Miller, Charles Gilson, J. Roy Hunt, George Webber
Film editor: James Smith
CAST: Carol Dempster (Joan Daisy Royle)
W.C. Fields (her father)
James Kirkwood (Calvin Clarke)
Harrison Ford (Fred Ketlar)
Marie Chambers (Adele Ketlar)
Paul Everton (George "Three-G" Baretta)
George Rigas (henchman)
Florence Auer (Baretta's girl)
Ida Waterman (Mrs. Clarke)
Alice Laidley (Clarke's fiancée)
Dorothea Love (Lola Neeson)
Dore Davidson (Elman)
Frank Allworth (Oliver)
Bobby Watson (Hofer)
Mary Meeker
Paul Gilbert
Alice Weaver and George White's Scandals dancers

A Lost and Found *Romance*

First published: www.jbkaufman.com, January 2013

In November 2012 I launched my official website, with a great deal of help from friend, tech wizard, and webmaster Barrett Morgan (who has also played a substantial role in the development of this book, among many other things). One of the site's features is a monthly column called "Movie of the Month," which is still going strong and has just passed 100 installments at this writing. It wasn't easy to single out just one of those entries to represent the entire "Movie of the Month" series in this anthology, but this particular one is one of my favorites, because of the film and because of the remarkable story behind its recovery and preservation.

    The Internet is not designed for long attention spans, and I make an effort to keep these columns down to a fairly short word count. The printed page is a different matter, and for this reprinting I've expanded the *Rafter Romance* piece considerably, adding more background information and details on the film. It's still not a very long essay, but it's more than twice the length of the original.

Thank you: Lee Tsiantis and Dennis Millay.

A LOST AND FOUND
ROMANCE

One of the happiest events of 2007 for film enthusiasts was the recovery of the six long-unavailable "RKO Lost and Found" films. Their story has been told elsewhere but, briefly, four of the films in question had been produced at RKO Radio Pictures under the supervision of legendary producer Merian C. Cooper, who left the studio in 1934. The terms of Cooper's severance were not settled until 1946, a good twelve years after his departure, and included his purchase of all rights to four of the films produced during his tenure. Because two of those films were remade in, respectively, 1937 and 1938, the remakes were also included in the package. Exactly why Cooper chose those *particular* films—and what he planned at the time to do with them—remains a mystery.[1] In any case, his acquisition was followed by more complications which plunged the six films into a legal limbo in which they could not be shown. Apart from a brief flurry of local television exposure in the late 1950s, the six films effectively disappeared from view for more than half a century.

For their rescue, we can thank Dennis Millay and Lee Tsiantis, who were at the time, respectively, TCM's programming director and Turner Broadcasting's corporate legal manager. Learning in 2006 of the peculiar legal status of these films, Millay and Tsiantis expended heroic efforts, first, to untangle the monumental legal snarl in which the films had been trapped for so many decades, and second, to track down and restore 35mm preservation elements for each title. This last was no mean feat; both the original negatives retained by RKO and the fine-grain masters made for Cooper in 1946 had been lost in the intervening years. Ultimately Millay and Tsiantis were successful in locating, and in one case reconstructing, high-quality prints of all six titles. The films were legally acquired by TCM and were unveiled in 2007, with special showings on the Turner channel and packaged in a special DVD collection.

Most film enthusiasts agreed that they were worth the wait. Granted that none of the six films qualified as lost classics (Cooper had reportedly negotiated in 1946 for John Ford's *The Lost Patrol*, a film whose revival *would* have been a major rediscovery), each one still offered special riches and pleasures of its own. One of the most enjoyable was the delightful pre-screwball comedy *Rafter Romance*, featuring Ginger Rogers in an early starring role.[2]

Having achieved some early recognition on the stage, Ginger Rogers had broken into the movies in 1929, appearing in a series of shorts and minor features. Some of her assignments were less than distinguished— the 1930 Paramount short *Office Blues*, in which she played a singing stenographer with a crush on her boss, is embarrassing to revisit today—but Ginger, ever the trouper, soldiered on, making the most of every opportunity for increased exposure. By 1933 she was steadily working her way toward top stardom, interspersing her leading roles in modest program pictures with lesser parts in major releases. Two of the latter, the hit musicals *42nd Street* and *Gold Diggers of 1933*, had earned her special attention—in particular *Gold Diggers*, which allowed her to show off her singing voice in the famous "We're in the Money" number. By the early summer of 1933 it was clear that this pert young comedienne, who could sing *and* dance *and* project an impish, biting wit, was headed for bigger things.

At this juncture RKO Radio cast Ginger in a top-billed role opposite Norman Foster, under the direction of William A. Seiter, in *Professional Sweetheart*. Her role was that of a radio singer, and oddly enough, Ginger—who had already proven her singing voice on both stage and screen—was dubbed, in her brief performance scenes, by another singer. Regardless, the experience of producing this film was a pleasant one for Ginger herself, who retained warm memories of William Seiter in later years: "Bill Seiter was a super guy, with a charming, adorable, witty, and engaging attitude toward his actors. I simply adored him. Some directors play out their own problems with their cast; others, like Bill, put personal issues aside and are charming and encouraging."[3] Encouraged by the film's enthusiastic reception, RKO reteamed Ginger, Norman Foster, and William Seiter for a followup feature, *Rafter Romance*, based on a recently published novel. Once again Ginger received top billing—and this time, notably, there were no singing or dancing scenes.

The gist of the film is in its plot situation: Ginger and Foster are two young people recently arrived in New York. They have never met, but both live in the same apartment house—a tenuous distinction, since both are in financial straits and behind on their rent. Their landlord, financially strapped himself, proposes that both of them can live in Foster's attic apartment—on an alternating basis. Foster, an aspiring painter who works a "day job" at night, can sleep in the apartment during the day; during the nighttime hours the apartment will be Ginger's. The landlord promises that they'll never have to meet, and is sure they'll both be happy with the arrangement. Of course both are extremely *un*happy with the arrangement, but are forced to accept it. Their instant dislike of one another is evident when each starts leaving nasty notes for the other; these soon lead to increasingly spiteful practical jokes.

Meanwhile, following the irresistible logic of the movies, Ginger and Foster meet on the street and begin a tentative romance. As hostilities escalate between the two anonymous roommates, romance continues to blossom between the young lovers. (The plot is loosely similar to that of *The Shop Around the Corner*, which Ernst Lubitsch would bring to the screen in 1940.) The two plot threads collide as the roommates' practical jokes become more extreme. In one scene, Foster's planned date with romantic partner Ginger is undone when roommate Ginger leaves his one good suit hanging under the shower head, drenching it with water.

This slender plot situation is given an engaging appeal by William Seiter, a reliable and versatile director whose sensitive handling of his actors was combined with a warm, subtle directorial style on the screen. Seiter has always been oddly underappreciated by the film community at large, but some discerning critics have been quick to point out the understated appeal of his films in a variety of genres. William K. Everson once wrote: "Seiter's work had taste and charm, and he had the happy knack of being able to present contemporary life and human foibles in dramatic or amusing ways, without distorting them or blowing them up to typically Hollywoodian proportions."[4] That knack is on display in *Rafter Romance* as the two leads play out their story, indulging in all-too-human idiosyncrasies, yet always holding the viewer's sympathy with an ingratiating charm.

Produced during the summer of 1933, *Rafter Romance* is technically a pre-Code film, but without any of the salacious content that some viewers

Encountering Ginger Rogers on the street in *Rafter Romance*, Norman Foster is anything but shy. © Turner Classic Movies.

expect from such a film (although that widespread simplistic understanding of the pre-Code period is largely a misinterpretation anyway; see "Footloose Widows in Havana," elsewhere in this volume). The film's basic situation—two strangers innocently "cohabiting"—may have skirted the limits of 1933 good taste, but so harmlessly (especially since both parties protest the idea!) that no one could have taken offense. If any part of this film did tempt the censors' scissors, it might have been the occasional shots of partially-clothed Ginger walking around the apartment—but these, too, are handled with impeccable taste.

Some fans of the pre-Code period are fond of another trait of these pictures: their unpredictable excursions into ethnic humor, some of it politically incorrect in today's world. *Rafter Romance*'s contribution is George Sidney, cast according to type as the Jewish landlord who sets the plot in motion. With his broad mannerisms and mangled English ("This ain't the Eckbaum Foundation for Indignant Females"), Sidney plays his specialty role to the hilt. But he's a thoroughly likable and sympathetic character, more a caring parent than a landlord, amiably solicitous toward his young charges. (In one scene, doubly remarkable in light of 1933 world events, Sidney finds his own son drawing swavastikas in chalk on a passageway wall—for "good luck"—and angrily erases them with his sleeve!)

And other beloved character players turn up, as well, in the supporting cast. Laura Hope Crews seems miscast as a perpetually tipsy would-be patron with designs on Foster, but Guinn "Big Boy" Williams lends his welcome presence as a rough but chivalrous cab driver. For many viewers, one highlight of the film is Robert Benchley's appearance in the cast. Benchley's initial venture into the movies in 1929 had been almost a fluke, a side pursuit separate from his writing career. In the Fox short *The Treasurer's Report* he had simply performed an informal sketch, of his own creation, lampooning pompous, befuddled after-dinner speakers. But Benchley on the screen had demonstrated a very real and very funny screen presence, and the short had achieved unexpected success and had brought offers for more of the same.[5] These in turn had led him into brief supporting roles in features, and by 1933 he had embarked on what would be a surprisingly long and prolific second career as a Hollywood character actor. As Ginger's lecherous boss in *Rafter Romance* he displays a hitherto unfamiliar persona, forever trying to maneuver Ginger into an intimate encounter, forever frustrated in the attempt. It's a character type we don't normally associate with Benchley, but he still manages to work in some of the bumbling-professor business that had served him so well in *The Treasurer's Report*.

With so many qualities going for it, and with the added benefit of that inexplicable warmth that Seiter seemed to inject into most of his films, *Rafter Romance* is a minor but thoroughly enjoyable little feature. For proof of its appeal we need look no further than the 1937 remake, *Living on Love*, which is also included in the "RKO Lost and Found" group. There's nothing *wrong* with *Living on Love*; it's a quite competently produced film with substantial talent both before and behind the camera. The two leads, James Dunn and Whitney Bourne, are certainly likable enough. Dunn, a prolific 1930s actor who had worked with talents as diverse as Shirley Temple and Erich von Stroheim, has a reckless, goofy charm that he can switch on, to good effect, during his comedy scenes. Bourne, a quiet beauty who is relatively little remembered today, proves herself more than capable of carrying a leading role. And, like the earlier film, *Living on Love* has its own complement of favorite character players in supporting roles. Tom Kennedy, the perennial tough mug of so many 1930s films, plays the taxi driver in this version; the script is revised to give him more comedy set-pieces than Guinn Williams had enjoyed in the original, and Kennedy makes the most of them. Franklin Pangborn replaces Robert Benchley as the heroine's lecherous boss and, cast against type, is remarkably convincing.

Too, *Living on Love* in 1937 had the advantage of timeliness. *Rafter Romance*, in a sense, had been ahead of its time; the screwball comedy as a genre simply had not existed in 1933. The intervening four years had changed all that with the release of *It Happened One Night*, *Libeled Lady*, *My Man Godfrey*, and other films now recognized as classics. The year 1937, in fact, saw a virtual deluge of sophisticated, offbeat romantic comedies: *The Awful Truth*, *Nothing Sacred*, *It's Love I'm After*, *Easy Living*, and numerous others. In the midst of this surge, it would have been surprising if RKO had *not* remade this story. *Living on Love* seems to revel in the moment: in one scene Dunn launches into a disquisition on the art of dunking a donut, instantly bringing to mind *It Happened One Night*. The two roommates' practical jokes on each other are far more elaborate than those in the earlier film and, in some cases, ingeniously clever.

A telling comparison between the two films can be found in their respective climactic scenes. Having set up an irresistible comedy situation—the starry-eyed lovers and bickering roommates who are, unwittingly, one and the same—both films are building toward the moment when the two principals discover each other's true identity. By all the rules of comedy, this must be the key moment in the story. And, in fact, both films do construct elaborate climactic sequences around this moment. But they do it in utterly different ways.

Let's look first at *Living on Love*. Dunn and Bourne have been out on a date—a modest affair, considering both their financial conditions—and now are returning home on foot. But neither can *really* return home, because neither has told the other about their respective living arrangements, and both are anxious to conceal them. As they approach the apartment house, each is at pains to keep the other from noticing it, and each pretends to be living in a more impressive building in the same neighborhood. Screenwriter Franklin Coen has some fun with this situation: both Dunn and Bourne dawdle around, pretend to be in no particular hurry, and generally stall—each waiting for the other to go home, so that *they* can go home. Before this has gone on very long, their conversation devolves into an argument. Tom Kennedy, overhearing the harsh words, gallantly steps in on Bourne's behalf and socks Dunn on the jaw, knocking him out cold. Bourne prevails on Kennedy to help her carry Dunn inside so that she can tend to his injury.

Thus the stage is set for the denouement: Dunn comes to in his own apartment, realizes that it's also *her* apartment, and instantly grasps the situation. How will he react? With barely suppressed glee he wanders

In the film's climactic scene, Ginger is none too happy with Foster—but instinctively shields him from "Big Boy" Williams' threats. © Turner Classic Movies

around the apartment, "discovering" men's clothing and other telltale signs of a male presence, and feigns shock and reproach. Poor Whitney squirms in embarrassment, proffering an explanation of the unorthodox living situation, while Dunn mischievously enjoys her discomfiture. It's a funny scene—but it's undone moments later when the script contrives to bring the rest of the story's characters flocking into the room, revealing the true situation to Bourne, and causing her to explode in anger when she realizes the trick Dunn has played on her. The scene gives way to a shouting match, this time involving *all* the characters. Bourne storms out of the apartment, Dunn pursues her—and then, abruptly, they decide that they love each other. In no time at all they're following a clergyman down the sidewalk and we're seeing the "End" title. It's a peremptory device, serving to wrap up the film in a tidy six reels, but it's less than convincing.

Now we turn to the original. In *Rafter Romance* the roles are reversed, and it's Ginger who first discovers the truth about the couple's respective identities. In this version Foster accompanies her to her company picnic, and the two sneak away from the rest of the group for

A LOST AND FOUND *ROMANCE*

a romantic interlude and miss the bus back to the city. Trying to carry Ginger across a stream, Foster slips and sprains his ankle, and the two hail a taxi to take them home. Ginger doesn't hear Foster's directions to the taxi driver, and during the trip home she's preoccupied with his injury, so she doesn't realize where they're going.

When the taxi arrives at its destination, then, all the pieces are in place for another denouement. Ginger helps Foster out of the taxi, looks up the stairs to the apartment building, and is thunderstruck when she realizes the truth. Like James Dunn in the later film, she instantly grasps the situation—but *unlike* Dunn's character, she doesn't instantly calculate a way to use it to her mischievous advantage. Instead, a range of shock and dismay is reflected in her face. Foster, for his part, has none of his later counterpart's embarrassment over revealing his home address. Indeed, he can't stop talking about it, and as Ginger helps him up flight after flight of stairs, he keeps up a silly running commentary as if he were an elevator operator. He's so talkative that he doesn't notice Ginger's spirits sinking lower as the couple climbs higher, further confirming her suspicions with every step.

They arrive at the apartment, and as they enter, Ginger maintains her silence—not to trip up Foster, but to hide her embarrassment and her desire to escape from an awkward situation as quickly as possible. Foster still can't stop talking; he cajoles Ginger into staying and binding up his ankle, and as she does, he holds forth in a diatribe about the "scrawny old maid" who has ruined his life. Cheerfully ignorant of his words' effect, he rattles on at length: "Oh, she's a blight! . . . I'd like to break her skinny neck!" Soon enough George Sidney is alerted to the simultaneous presence of both roommates in the apartment. He bustles into the room, protesting loudly, and for the first time Foster himself realizes the truth.

From this point on, the two films make for a fascinating side-by-side comparison. In strict terms of continuity, they're identical: the arrival of the landlord, followed closely by most of the other principals in the cast; the revelation of the truth and subsequent shouting match; the heroine's exasperated exit, with the hero close on her heels; the argument outside, suddenly and romantically resolved. But what a difference! Whitney Bourne in 1937 is strong, independent, indignant. Ginger Rogers in 1933 has the same qualities, but somehow adds a layer of vulnerability; we *know* she could tear Foster to ribbons if she chose, but we sympathize with her when she dissolves into tears instead. William Seiter's direction of the scene blends beautifully with this version of the character. The climactic episode in *Living on Love* is played strictly for comedy; director Lew Landers never misses an opportunity for a laugh. Seiter in *Rafter Romance* is willing to sacrifice a few of those laughs in favor of an undercurrent of tenderness. *Living on Love* is a pleasant, diverting comedy; *Rafter Romance* lingers in the memory after the final fadeout, its laughs tinged with an understated sweetness.

That we even have the luxury of *seeing* these films, and indulging in these comparisons, is a testament to the invaluable gift that the "RKO Lost and Found" package represents. Film enthusiasts everywhere owe a debt of gratitude to Dennis Millay, Lee Tsiantis, and the Turner company for rescuing yet another chapter of our cinematic legacy and restoring it to view.

Notes

1. In this connection, it's perhaps worth noting that Dorothy Jordan had originally been announced as the star of *Rafter Romance* [Ralph Wilk, "A Little from 'Lots'," *Film Daily*, 21 February 1933, p. 7]. Ultimately Ginger Rogers played the role, while Dorothy Jordan played a featured role in *One Man's Journey* (another of the "Lost and Found" titles) instead. In the meantime she also married Merian Cooper, and shortly afterward retired from the screen. One doesn't want to indulge in too much speculation, but it's possible that Cooper's interest in *One Man's Journey* and *Rafter Romance* had something to do with his wife's appearance in one, and her marginal connection with the other.

2. For the record, the other 1933–34 titles were *Double Harness*, starring William Powell and Ann Harding; *One Man's Journey*, starring Lionel Barrymore; and *Stingaree*, with Irene Dunne and Richard Dix. *Living on Love* (1937), the remake of *Rafter Romance*, and *A Man to Remember* (1938), the remake of *One Man's Journey*, rounded out the package. *A Man to Remember*, the film that proved most elusive in the course of Millay and Tsiantis' rescue operation, had been singled out by the *New York Times* in 1938 as one of the ten best films of the year. The reconstruction job was *Double Harness*, which restored two and a half missing minutes, from a nitrate dupe negative at the CNC Archives in Bois d'Arcy, France, to the otherwise complete television negative. TCM press release, 2007.

3. Ginger Rogers, *Ginger: My Story*, p. 119. It's worth noting that *Professional Sweetheart* was not the first cinematic meeting of Ginger Rogers and Norman Foster. They had shared some scenes in Paramount's *Young Man of Manhattan* (1930).

4. Everson, *American Silent Film*, p. 146.

5. For an excellent account of Benchley's career in short subjects, see Maltin, *The Great Movie Shorts*, pp. 165–71.

Rafter Romance

RKO Radio, 1 September 1933
Copyright © 14 September 1933 by RKO-Radio Pictures, Inc. (LP4120)
8 reels

Director: William A. Seiter
Screenplay: H.W. Hanemann and Sam Mintz, adapted by Glenn Tryon from the novel by John Wells
Art directors: Van Nest Polglase and John J. Hughes
Camera: David Abel (camera operator: Joe Biroc, assisted by Charles Bohny)
Music director: Max Steiner
Film editor: James B. Morley
Assistant director: Doran Cox
CAST: Ginger Rogers (Mary Carroll)
Norman Foster (Jack Bacon)
George Sidney (Eckbaum)
Robert Benchley (H. Harrington Hubbell)
Laura Hope Crews (Elise Peabody Worthington Smythe)
Guinn "Big Boy" Williams (Fritzie)
Sidney Miller (Julius Eckbaum)
Ferike Boros (Rosie Eckbaum)

Living on Love

RKO Radio, 12 November 1937
Copyright © 12 November 1937 by RKO Radio Pictures, Inc. (LP7579)
6 reels

Director: Lew Landers
Screenplay: Franklin Coen, based on the novel *Rafter Romance* by John Wells
Art directors: Van Nest Polglase and Feild M. Gray
Camera: Nicholas Musuraca
Film editor: Harry Marker
Assistant director: Sammy Ruman
CAST: James Dunn (Gary Martin)
Whitney Bourne (Mary Wilson)
Joan Woodbury (Edith Crumwell)
Solly Ward (Eli West)
Tom Kennedy (Pete Ryan)
Franklin Pangborn (Ogilvie O. Oglethorpe)
Kenneth Terrell, James Fawcett (Ghonoff brothers)
Chester Clute (Jessup)
Evelyn Carter Carrington (Madame La Valley)
Etta McDaniel (Lizbeth)
Harry Bowen (taxi driver)
Otto Hoffman (Alex)

Footloose Widows in Havana: The Changing Face of Warner Bros. Comedy, 1926–1933

Not previously published.

A new essay, unveiled here for the first time, but pulling together some threads that I've been following for some time. In a sense this piece is an extreme expansion of the program note I wrote for Footloose Widows *as part of the "Funny Ladies" retrospective at the Giornate in 2002. That was my introduction to the film, and it was a delightful discovery and immediately suggested a kinship between this and some later and more familiar titles. The ensuing research led to more discoveries, which are now encapsulated in this essay.*

I've indicated elsewhere in this volume that Paramount is one of my favorite major studios. The other is Warner Bros. Each of the majors had its own distinctive identity, and I find the Warners identity irresistible, for reasons that I hope will be evident in this essay. And even beyond the specifics of Warner Bros., researching and writing this piece has reinforced for me just how endless is the study of classic films. One road always leads to another. We'll never know everything there is to know about the classic era—there will always be new discoveries waiting for us, endlessly fascinating, captured on film (or some other visual medium) for all time.

Thank you: Paolo Cherchi Usai, Piera Patat and Livio Jacob, David Robinson (Le Giornate del Cinema Muto), Mike Mashon (Library of Congress); Nancy Kauffman; and Noelle Carter, Sandra Joy Lee, Brett Service, and the staff of the Warner Bros. Archives, School of Cinematic Arts, University of Southern California, Los Angeles.

FOOTLOOSE WIDOWS IN HAVANA

THE CHANGING FACE OF WARNER BROS. COMEDY, 1926–1933

The rise of the Warner Bros. studio from modest low-budget production company to major Hollywood powerhouse, within a few short years during the 1920s, is one of the great success stories in film history. It was not accomplished without heroic effort, boundless ambition, perilous risk-taking, and shrewd maneuvering on the part of the Warners themselves and their associates. And no small part of their eventual success was due to a canny collective ability to read their audience, and the culture at large, and to respond quickly and appropriately. If a trend was in the offing, the Warner filmmakers could spot it from a distance and anticipate it on the screen. Ultimately they were able to read the times accurately enough to create their *own* trends. This sensitivity to popular taste was rewarded with increasing dividends at the box office.

There can be no better illustration than the presence of Louise Fazenda at the studio in the 1920s. For most silent-film enthusiasts, the mention of Louise Fazenda evokes images of the slapstick comedies of

Keystone. After an apprenticeship at Universal, Fazenda joined the Keystone forces in 1915 and plunged into the studio's knockabout world with gusto, appearing in dozens of one- and two-reel shorts. She cultivated the persona of a gawky, ungainly country girl and demonstrated her willingness to indulge in violently strenuous physical comedy. As *Variety* put it, "She was dragged by horses, tossed from heights, and otherwise engaged in gymnastics no other comedienne dared undertake."[1] When Mack Sennett abandoned Keystone and formed a new studio, Fazenda went along as a member of his stock company, reprising her awkward yokel character in both shorts and features.

But by the early 1920s Sennett's brand of comedy was being overtaken by more sophisticated styles, and Fazenda had moved on. She abandoned the movies altogether for a short stint in vaudeville, then, in 1922, returned to the screen transformed. The new Louise Fazenda was a revelation: still a comedienne, but a versatile one who could hold her own in subtle, refined comedy, and even an occasional role in a straight dramatic picture.

Her reinvention of her professional self coincided with the rise of the Warner Bros. studio. During the early 1920s the Warner brothers were embarking on the effort to establish their company as a major Hollywood studio—a goal they would successfully realize by the end of the decade. Louise Fazenda's acting roles took her to a variety of movie studios during these years, but she turned up with increasing frequency in Warner Bros. features.[2] In *The Gold Diggers* (1923), a film that marked a significant milestone in Warners history,[3] she played the key role of Mabel. She appeared as a kind-hearted prostitute in *This Woman* (1924) and as a wisecracking chorus girl in *A Broadway Butterfly* (1925). By March 1926, then, when she was cast in the lead in *Footloose Widows*, Louise Fazenda was a long way from Keystone.

Too, *Footloose Widows* was a very different kind of comedy. Its nominal source was Beatrice Burton's serialized story "Footloose," syndicated in newspapers during the summer of 1925. "Footloose" was the story of a young widow whose husband had killed himself over her infidelity. Coolly setting out to trap herself a rich second husband, she was herself fleeced by a con man and, left without resources, was forced to live by her wits. After this teasingly sensational opening, "Footloose" devolved into a rather conventional romance in which the chastened girl came to appreciate the hometown suitor who really loved her. "I consider this story a very poor buy," sniffed a Warners reader. "The character of the woman is very unsympathetic and is confined to a number of flirtatious incidents until she finally succeeds in annexing herself a middle-aged husband."[4]

But Warner Bros. did buy the rights to the property, and transformed it into something utterly unlike Burton's original story. This transformation was the work of the scenario writer, Darryl Francis Zanuck. Having joined the studio staff in 1924, Zanuck was a young dynamo who would, through his scripts and his production supervision, play an important role in establishing the popular identity of Warner Bros. The indelible image that would come to define Warners films during the early 1930s—the world of ruthless gangsters, tough-talking newspaper editors, and hard-boiled dames; of raw, vivid stories ripped from the headlines—was largely his creation.

In the mid-1920s, Zanuck was already planting the seeds of that image. The very element of "Footloose" that had so repulsed the studio reader, the amoral protagonist and her shameless pursuit of a rich, gullible victim, was precisely what *did* appeal to Zanuck. He had joined the Warners staff after *The Gold Diggers* was already produced and playing in theaters, but he openly embraced the spirit of the film and of the original Avery Hopwood play on which it was based. Zanuck's protagonist might be a "gold digger,"[5] cynically exploiting her feminine charms to prey on rich older men, but he would not make excuses, sentimentalize, or moralize. Instead he would *celebrate* her exploits and play them for laughs. The sympathetic, street-smart chorine or working girl would become a familiar movie type in the '20s and '30s, at Warners and elsewhere, and audiences would root for her as she allowed some self-important older man, who probably had it coming anyway, to make a fool of himself over her.

In Zanuck's hands, Burton's "Footloose" became Warner Bros.' *Footloose Widows*, a lighthearted, cheerfully satirical comedy. Zanuck retained a few elements from the published story, but radically rearranged them and supplemented them with a full complement of his own ideas. Now, instead of one protagonist, there were two: wisecracking, cynical Flo, played by Louise Fazenda, and lovely Marion, played by Jacqueline Logan, a former *Follies* beauty who had established herself in the movies at Paramount and Fox during the early 1920s. Neither Flo nor Marion was actually a widow; instead they were models in a New York fashion house, and it was Logan's fetching appearance, *modeling* widow's weeds, that helped to set the plot in motion.[6]

At first glance the two leads' roles seem somewhat unkindly written, with a clear line of demarcation between The Pretty One and The Funny One. As we see them on the screen, however, there's never any doubt that Louise Fazenda is firmly in control of the situation and the film. Jacqueline Logan, for her part, is far more than a pretty face and complements Fazenda so well that one wonders why the two were

Louise Fazenda and Jacqueline Logan, as the title characters in *Footloose Widows*, exhibit a knowing confidence as they go after their objectives. Douglas Gerrard is properly nervous. © Warner Bros. Courtesy George Eastman Museum.

not teamed more often in later films. The butt of the humor is the fashion shop's proprietor, Sir Grover Dunn, played by Douglas Gerrard as the ultimate pompous, stuffy Englishman. Strutting and preening, possessed of a ridiculous open-mouthed laugh when he's pleased with himself, forever uttering (in a dialogue title) a trademark "Yoo-hoo-hoo," Gerrard's performance is an obnoxious delight. He is, it seems, just asking for someone to deflate his colossal ego.

He doesn't have to wait long. After several unsuccessful attempts to date Logan, he hits on the idea of inviting the two models to a party at his apartment, and magnanimously offers them their choice of clothing from the store—just for the evening. The entire luxurious inventory of the shop is theirs for the borrowing. This is the opportunity Fazenda has been waiting for. Sweetly accepting Gerrard's offer, dutifully noting the directions to his apartment, she helps herself and Logan to large armloads of gowns and frocks from the rack, and piles them all into a taxi—then tears up Gerrard's card and heads for the railroad station. Before Gerrard has any idea what's happened, the two "widows" are in Florida, equipped with fabulous wardrobes and on the prowl for at least one rich husband.

Their adventures at the Florida resort hotel occupy five reels of this seven-reel feature, and run the gamut of comedy styles. Fazenda wastes no time discovering that their fellow guests include a self-made millionaire, "J.A. Smith," and engineering Logan's meeting with him—unaware that there are actually *two* J.A. Smiths at the hotel, and setting the stage for an extended series of mistaken-identity gags. Logan accidentally meets the Smith who really is rich (Jason Robards), and finds herself instantly attracted to him; but, unaware of his identity, reluctantly goes along with Fazenda's plan and plays up to the *other* Smith (John Miljan)—who is, in fact, a penniless con man. Zanuck and director Roy Del Ruth wring a variety of comedy situations from this slender premise.

Much of the humor is subtle situation comedy—conveyed largely by visual means, without relying on wordy titles—but, when the situation warrants, the film doesn't shy away from out-and-out slapstick. Hard-pressed for a discreet way to initiate a conversation with Miljan, Fazenda simply lies in wait for him on his daily promenade, trips him, and sends him pitching headlong across the patio. She and Logan pounce on their now unconscious victim and half-drag, half-carry him up to their room, ostensibly to revive him. When they reach the crowded elevator, the operator is nowhere to be found. Fazenda doesn't bother to wait, but simply commandeers the elevator herself, and the floor indicator describes a frantic trajectory that leaves the other passengers sprawled, dazed, and reeling when the elevator doors open again.

One notable comedy highlight occurs in reel 5, when Fazenda relates to Miljan the (spurious) story of Logan's widowhood. Her tale is a broad burlesque of the situation in Burton's original story: Logan's husband returns home unexpectedly on Christmas Eve, to find his wife in the arms of a supposed lover—in reality "only her brother, whom Ludwig had never seen before"—and is driven to suicide. The story is told as a flashback, and Logan's imaginary husband is played by none other than Mack Swain, the rotund Keystone comic who was currently enjoying a comeback (having recently been featured in Chaplin's *The Pilgrim* and *The Gold Rush*). By contrast with the subtle wit of some other scenes, Swain plays this one as wildly exaggerated farce, streaming tears and all. It's an enjoyable and completely gratuitous interlude, clearly inserted for its own sake.[7]

Inevitably, Gerrard shows up in Florida in the penultimate reel, looking for the ladies and, more urgently, his dresses. Fazenda's bold caper seems doomed, as Gerrard threatens to publicly expose the "widows" as thieves and gold diggers—which, of course, they are. But Fazenda isn't finished yet. Now, in one of her most remarkable scenes in the picture, she turns her seductive charms on Gerrard. Considering the way her character has been written and played up to this point, Fazenda's seduction scene is surprisingly effective. It has its effect on Gerrard: instantly forgetting his earlier humiliation at the ladies' hands, he allows himself to be lured into a private room. Once he's there, Fazenda quickly cuts the phone line, locks him in, and is on her way out the door before Gerrard realizes he's been duped *again*. His ensuing scene of comic humiliation is even more extreme than the first one. Discovering the locked door and the lifeless telephone, his panic mounting, he tears the phone from the wall, smashes furniture, and pounds the door ever more frantically—pausing now and then to bellow: "Thank God—I'm still an English gentleman!"

Meanwhile Logan finds Robards and makes up with him. Needless to say, all ends happily—for Logan and Robards, for Fazenda and the comic love interest (Neely Edwards) who has been dogging her since her arrival in Florida, and even for Gerrard, who is reimbursed for his loss and stalks out of the premises with as much dignity as he can still muster.

The audience, too, has every reason for good cheer by the end of this film. *Footloose Widows* is not a cinematic "first" in any way, but for viewers unfamiliar with the Warner Bros. output of the 1920s, this film provides a pleasant introduction. Barely three years into Warners' expansion program,[8] *Footloose Widows* announces an unmistakable studio identity: smart, savvy, cheerfully cynical. It's essentially a new kind of screen comedy. Here the rough-and-tumble slapstick of Keystone is not forgotten[9]—Louise Fazenda is the top-billed star, after all, and Mack Swain plays his extended cameo with broad, reckless gusto. But these elements are incorporated into a subtly crafted comedy with a more urban sensibility, set in a world of slick operators, con men, and shrewd young women who are fully capable of wrapping rich men around their fingers and squeezing them dry. As we watch this film, it's impossible to miss the point: by 1926, Warner Bros. is already Warner Bros.

This was a time of bustling activity at the studio, of course, and one of Warners' most significant concurrent activities was its embrace of talking pictures. By the time *Footloose Widows* opened in June 1926, the studio had already entered into a flourishing partnership with Western Electric to form the Vitaphone corporation. The following year, the release of the milestone talkie *The Jazz Singer* would help to catapult Warners into a league with the most prestigious studios in Hollywood. They cemented that status in 1928–29 with their acquisition of First National, absorbing that studio's production facilities and extensive theater chain into their existing assets. By decade's end, Warner Bros.

had succeeded in establishing itself as an industry leader and was busily engaged in turning out a full slate of sound films. In the process, the studio had largely reinvented its own image and transformed the face of American movies in general.

An important part of Warners' new sound-film program was the production of musicals. *The Jazz Singer* in 1927 had arguably qualified as a musical, and Warners had soon moved on with still more ambitious efforts: revues and backstage stories featuring elaborate production numbers, many filmed partly or wholly in Technicolor. An unlikely star had emerged from this new specialty genre: Winnie Lightner. Brash, raucous, and irrepressible, Lightner had made her name in vaudeville in the 1920s and had been snapped up for the screen, along with other stage performers, in Vitaphone musical shorts. From there it was a short jump to features, and when Warners remade *The Gold Diggers* as a musical in 1929, retitling it *Gold Diggers of Broadway*, Lightner was cast in the role of Mable [sic]—the role that had been played by Louise Fazenda in the 1923 silent. Physically and stylistically the two actresses were vastly dissimilar, but in the brash new world of Warners musicals, Lightner clicked instantly with audiences. *Gold Diggers of Broadway* was an immense hit, and Lightner was one of its top attractions—"hurtling through it all like a very noisy comet," as historian Richard Barrios has written.[10] Practically overnight, Warners had a new star.

The studio lost no time in mounting new followup vehicles for her. Her unique screen persona suggested a very specific showcase. Not for Winnie the plaintive romantic ballad or the heartfelt torch song; she was at her best when belting out raucous comedy numbers like "Singing in the Bathtub," a pointed parody of MGM's recent hit "Singin' in the Rain." This was her featured number in Warners' all-star revue *The Show of Shows*, released a scant three months after *Gold Diggers of Broadway*, and once again Lightner scored a direct hit with reviewers and audiences. More films quickly followed in 1930: *She Couldn't Say No*, featuring Lightner in a dramatic role as a blues singer, and *Hold Everything*, teaming her with Joe E. Brown.[11]

In the continuing search for followup vehicles, coincidentally or not, the studio cast Lightner in another Louise Fazenda role: a loose remake of *Footloose Widows*. The story was adapted as a musical and retitled *The Life of the Party*. Once again the script was the work of Darryl Zanuck, writing under the name Melville Crossman,[12] and once again Roy Del Ruth was the director. In adapting the story, Zanuck didn't *change* the original script so much as build around it. In terms of its basic plot, *The Life of the Party* is essentially identical to *Footloose Widows*, but Zanuck cannily inserts new elements to exploit the use of sound, the use of Technicolor, and, most tellingly, the idiosyncratic talents of the film's leading players. Foremost among these, of course, are the two gold-digging protagonists. Winnie Lightner is nothing like Louise Fazenda, but fulfills her role in the story: the scheming comic who drives the plot. In place of Jacqueline Logan, the film gives us Irene Delroy—a Broadway beauty who, like Lightner, had some singing and dancing experience on the stage, but whose career in the movies would be brief.

Thus, the opening scenes of *The Life of the Party* are actually a tacked-on prologue, featuring Lightner and Delroy not as fashion models but as song pluggers in a music store.[13] This section of the film makes full use of the sound-film medium, with music and with fast, slangy dialogue, as the pair endeavor to sell song sheets to a crowd of apathetic customers, under the watchful eye of their boss (an unbilled Eddie Kane). *The Life of the Party* was planned in the spring of 1930 as a musical, with a full complement of songs, and was before the cameras by early June.[14] But production coincided with an industry-wide recognition, during the course of the year, that musical films were rapidly wearing out their welcome with audiences. Most of the major studios responded to this sudden shift by drastically reducing the musical content of their films, and Warner Bros. was no exception. By autumn, when the finished film was ready for release, it retained exactly *one* song, and Winnie the song-plugger belts it out in this opening sequence: a characteristically broad comedy number titled "Poison Ivy" ("He got a Poison Ivy/Instead of a clinging vine").

Otherwise, the sequence sets the tone for the rest of the film with a barrage of boisterous dialogue. Lightner hails the passersby with a spiel hawking the store's selection of song hits, all of which seem to be taken from recent Warner Bros. movies (including several that had starred Lightner herself). Irene Delroy, somewhat more demure—and deprived of any songs to sing—simply plays the piano to accompany Lightner during *her* number. The sequence also introduces a customer who is clearly the ladies' number-one fan, LeMaire the modiste, played by Charles Judels. His fixation on Delroy amounts to an hysterical mania, and when the store owner objects to his disruption of business, Judels stages an epic tantrum—the first of several, as it turns out. He tosses song sheets about the store in a blizzard of paper, smashes a vase, and manifests a special fondness for breaking glass by shattering the plate-glass window at the front of the store. In no time at all the ladies are fired. Needing to find new jobs right away, they go to work for Judels in his fashion store, and at this point *The Life of the Party* settles into the plot trajectory established four years earlier in *Footloose Widows*.

Now a comparison of the two films becomes a fascinating study in adaptation. In crafting *The Life of the Party*, Zanuck and Del Ruth stick

Retribution, and Charles Judels, are about to catch up with Winnie Lightner and Irene Delroy in *The Life of the Party*. © Warner Bros. Courtesy George Eastman Museum.

closely to the formula that had already worked in 1926, down to repeating modest sight gags and dialogue titles from *Footloose Widows*. Some of the variations are slight, and some are simply playful ("J.A. Smith" in the earlier film becomes "A.J. Smith" in the new one). On the other hand, Zanuck and Del Ruth are fully prepared to insert major detours that exploit the trappings of their medium. We've already observed their opening sequence, seemingly added simply to capitalize on sound by means of music and snappy dialogue. Now, in the second reel, Technicolor gets its due in the form of an extended fashion show. Filmmakers of the 1920s had been quick to discover that trends in feminine fashion lent themselves well to color photography, and fashion shows had become a favorite subject for Technicolor films.[15] Now, since their story already includes a fashion show, Zanuck and Del Ruth take the opportunity to tease out the proceedings far beyond the demands of strict necessity. By the time Irene Delroy makes her head-turning appearance in widow's weeds, the Technicolor cameras have already been treated to a long parade of elegantly gowned models.[16]

But the most conspicuous departures in this new film are those tailored to the strengths of the leading players. Notable among these, at this point in the story, is Charles Judels as LeMaire. This character is the counterpart to Douglas Gerrard's character in the earlier film (and inherits Gerrard's chronic "Yoo-hoo," this time audibly), but if Gerrard's English dressmaker is pompous and laughable, Judels' French dressmaker is volatile and frenzied, a human volcano. Judels had long been established in vaudeville as a player who specialized in a range of dialects—not actually speaking Italian, French, or the other languages of his multinational gallery of characters, but spouting a stream of gibberish that *sounded* authentic to the situation. He had appeared in some silent films, but his movie career really took hold with the arrival of sound, when his performance specialty could be exploited. (Many of today's viewers may know him best from Walt Disney's *Pinocchio*, in which he provided the voices of both the Cockney Coachman and the Italian Stromboli.[17])

As the excitable LeMaire in *The Life of the Party*, Judels is an unbridled ham. There's nothing subtle about his attraction to Irene Delroy in this second reel; Lightner teases him with compliments Delroy has supposedly paid him, and by the time he has arranged for his models to attend the "party" at his apartment that evening, he's so excited he can't stand it. He improvises an extended little dance, and spouts a torrent of mock French. (An internal studio document addressed his synthetic dialect: "Note: Mr. Judel [sic] only fakes French—nothing authentic."[18]) And all this pales beside his later discovery that the ladies have tricked him and will *not* be attending the party. This discovery is the occasion for another tantrum that dwarfs the first one: an unrestrained Judels tears off his clothes, smashes furniture (his own, this time), and bellows at length in his rage.

Meanwhile the other strand of the story is proceeding according to plan. Lightner and Delroy pile into a taxi with their lavish new wardrobe; Delroy is, like Jacqueline Logan, ignorant of the plan and starts to hand Judels' card to the taxi driver; Lightner tosses away the card and directs the driver to Pennsylvania Station instead. At this point Lightner reveals the ladies' actual destination: not Florida, but Havana. This change serves to up the ante considerably from what we've seen in *Footloose Widows*. Florida was and is a popular vacation spot, but Cuba, in those pre-Revolution years, had a special aura all its own: glamorous, exciting, perhaps slightly dangerous—and, during Prohibition, a more-or-less convenient destination offering the promise of legal alcohol.[19] The exotic connotations of a trip to Havana lend a daring spirit to the proceedings.

Having suggested that atmosphere, *The Life of the Party* makes little of it, but continues along its predetermined course. Once again the "widows" check into the hotel, set their sights on a resident millionaire, and mistakenly pursue a penniless pretender with the same name (played by John Davidson). Once again, Delroy tries to cooperate with the plan but falls for what she and Lightner believe is the wrong man (Jack Whiting, another import from the musical stage). Once again, desperate to catch the attention of the man they *think* is a prize catch, they resort to tripping him in the hotel courtyard—producing a rather tame fall, compared to that in the earlier film—and haul their unconscious victim up to their room. The crux of the story remains the same as in 1926: a sham romance between two swindlers, each convinced that the other is fabulously wealthy. And, like Louise Fazenda, Winnie Lightner has an admirer of her own, this time in the person of Charles Butterworth. Butterworth was new to the movies in 1930, and his patented brand of vaguely addled non-sequitur dialogue was well suited to the talkies. Consequently he assumes a far greater proportion of screen time than Neely Edwards had enjoyed in *Footloose Widows*.

As in the opening reels, the most striking departures are those tailored to the leading players. Zanuck and Del Ruth display an ingenious resourcefulness here: *The Life of the Party* had been planned as a vehicle for Winnie Lightner the musical-comedy star, and was already in progress when Warners decided to turn its back on musicals. In mid-production, Winnie Lightner the musical-comedy star became Winnie Lightner the roughhouse comedienne. Most of her songs having been eliminated from the script, the filmmakers compensated with a surplus of comedy bits for her. They missed no opportunity for broad humor: like Louise Fazenda before her, Lightner is so impatient to hustle the bogus "Smith" upstairs that she commandeers the elevator and takes the other passengers on a reckless ride. Much of the newly added comedy content is dialogue-heavy: in a later scene Lightner and Delroy entertain Davidson in the hotel dining room. He tries to impress them with his knowledge of European capitals, but Lightner's punch lines make it clear that she has no idea what he's talking about.

The most striking departure from *Footloose Widows* occurs late in the film. Here the Charles Butterworth character is portrayed as a horse breeder with a horse entered in an upcoming race. Lightner becomes convinced that the horse may actually be a champion and, on a hunch, bets the ladies' entire bankroll on the horse. On the day of the race, a crisis: Butterworth's jockey is drunk and all the other jockeys are afraid to ride the horse, so the horse is out of the race. Naturally Lightner, who has never been near a horse in her life, volunteers to take the jockey's place. Considering the constraints that still hampered sound-film production in 1930, the race sequence is smoothly done, combining smooth tracking shots of the pack of horses, medium shots of individual horses and riders, and process shots of Lightner broadly clowning on "horseback." Of course the race ends disastrously for both Lightner and her bankroll, and the ladies are once again penniless, staking their hopes on what they think will be Delroy's lifesaving marriage of convenience.

On cue, Charles Judels shows up at the hotel, recognizes his old friend Davidson, learns of the impending nuptials, and spills the beans about the runaway gold diggers. Hastening to the ladies' room, he confronts *them* with the truth about Delroy's intended. Lightner responds like Louise Fazenda in 1926, turning her seductive charms on Judels in order to buy time while she and Delroy escape. This time the seduction is mostly verbal: Lightner waxes poetic about moonlight and romantic Havana, and once again Judels is simple-minded enough to fall for it. Moments later, realizing that he's been duped again, he embarks on a tantrum designed to surpass not only Douglas Gerrard's behavior in 1926 but also Judels' own earlier outbursts in *this* film. Roaring, demolishing furniture, smashing *several* mirrors this time, he stages a rampant display of temperament as the camera simply settles back to watch.

Meanwhile, the ladies start to make their getaway but are interrupted by Arthur Hoyt, Whiting's secretary (the equivalent of the role he had also played in *Footloose Widows*), who explains that *this* Mr. Smith is genuinely a millionaire. Instantly they shift gears and make for the corridor outside Whiting's room, where Lightner prevails on Delroy to fake yet another "fainting spell." (Delroy has a mildly pre-Code line of dialogue here: "But Flo, I've laid on my back on every floor in this hotel!") Ultimately all the loose ends are tied up, all the characters are satisfied or at least appeased—Judels departing the premises with a relatively subdued exit line: "I'm glad I did not lose my temper!"—and the film ends happily.

The Life of the Party opened in late 1930 to a successful run in theaters. Critical reaction was mixed but generally positive. Once again Darryl Zanuck, Roy Del Ruth, and the Warners team had crafted a new piece of screen entertainment, based on the same story, but utterly unlike *Footloose Widows*. If the result seems, to our eyes, a step backward from the crisp, witty comedy of the earlier film, it's important to remember that the filmmakers were operating in the moment. Their task was to tailor their product to the demands of the box office at that specific time. The point is reinforced by their pivot in mid-production, transforming *The Life of the Party* from a large-scale Technicolor musical, as first planned, to a very different kind of film—still Technicolor, still featuring handsome sets, but replacing song numbers with boisterous, largely verbal comedy. The wisdom of their strategy is evidenced by the success of the film: in autumn

1930, with audiences evincing a sudden aversion to musicals, *The Life of the Party* was exactly what the doctor ordered.

We know through hindsight, of course, that that public distaste for musicals didn't last forever—that a few groundbreaking musicals did appear, to reasonable business, in 1931–32, and that the genre came roaring back with a vengeance in 1933 with *42nd Street*. That dramatic comeback was courtesy of the Warners studio itself, and by mid-1933 Warners found itself in a world very different from that of the autumn of 1930. For one thing, the country had settled crushingly into the depths of the Great Depression. Widespread unemployment, breadlines, and desperate financial straits were now an everyday fact of life in America, and the newly elected Franklin Roosevelt was hastily assembling a slate of social programs to try to bolster the fortunes of ordinary citizens. Warner Bros., paradoxically, found itself in a position to benefit from these hard times. The milieu of street-level, blue-collar edginess that Darryl Zanuck had been at such pains to establish came into full flower during these years, and Warners became the studio of the common man, the voice of the people. Its hard-edged crime films and flashy musicals made no effort to run away from the harsh realities of everyday American life, but did reach out a sympathetic hand and attempt to lift the spirits of hurting moviegoers.

They made that attempt *without* the presence of Zanuck himself, who had left the studio abruptly in April 1933 after a heated dispute with Harry Warner.[20] Roy Del Ruth, the other creative force behind *Footloose Widows* and *The Life of the Party*, remained at Warner Bros.—but in the spring of 1933, when the studio decided to take up this story yet again, he was occupied with other projects. As a result, the new film, *Havana Widows*, was to all appearances an original idea, produced by an all-new creative team. The director this time was Ray Enright, himself no stranger to Warners filmmaking, having been a reliable staff director since 1927. The script was in the hands of another Warners veteran, Earl Baldwin, and it was Baldwin's name alone that appeared in the screen writing credits—no mention of Darryl Zanuck, let alone Beatrice Burton or any previous story.

And, in fairness, the basic story idea had been adapted so heavily between 1926 and 1933 that *Havana Widows* did count as a largely original effort. Once again the filmmakers tailored their material to the highly specific world of mid-1933, when production began. All that remained of the earlier iterations was the skeleton of the plot: two young ladies escape, with the unwitting help of a gullible male admirer, to an exotic location where they hope to improve their financial lot. Almost everything else in the story was new.

To begin with, the protagonists in this story were not fashion models or song pluggers. The Warners onscreen world had transformed radically since 1930, and now the heroines were cynical, wisecracking chorus girls like those in *42nd Street* (which had opened to overwhelming business in March 1933) or *Gold Diggers of 1933* (which had just finished shooting in mid-April). But these chorines were not performing in a glittering, sensational production like the fictional shows in those two major films; instead they were dancing in a cheap, tawdry burlesque hall for meager wages.[21] To make matters worse, one of them was fined in the opening scene for scratching her back while onstage, while the other was laid off for a week for refusing to appear in the altogether for a men's "smoker" on the side. The film was originally planned with Aline MacMahon and Glenda Farrell in the leads;[22] later MacMahon was dropped from the cast, Farrell replaced her in the Louise Fazenda/Winnie Lightner role as the instigator of the ladies' scheme, and Joan Blondell, who had been steadily building her star status at Warners, was teamed with her as The Pretty One. And unlike Jacqueline Logan and Irene Delroy, the designated beauties in the earlier films, Blondell was the top-billed star in this one.

Second, Blondell's and Farrell's racket in this film has nothing to do with masquerading as widows, or trying to trap rich husbands. Here, a far more direct and cunning scheme falls in their laps. As they sit in their apartment, bemoaning their impoverished state, they receive a visitor: a former fellow chorine (an unbilled Noel Francis), now bedecked in jewels and sporting a Russian wolfhound and a chauffeured limousine. Her secret, confided in pretentiously cultured tones: she has been to Havana, hooked a rich married man, and sued him for breach of promise. No need to concern herself with such annoying trifles as actually marrying the victim; through this breach-of-promise angle she has tapped directly into his wealth. A sharp lawyer named Duffy, she tells the ladies, has handled the whole affair and can do the same for them. The solution to their financial worries is clear: set sail for Havana and entrap a rich sucker (or two) in a breach-of-promise suit.

And this leads to another point of departure from *Footloose Widows* and *Life of the Party*: Blondell and Farrell, having nothing to do with the fashion industry, will not be absconding with fabulous wardrobes. All they really need is enough money for passage to Havana, and living expenses to tide them over. And to provide this seed money, their unwitting benefactor is not a volatile modiste but Blondell's off-and-on boyfriend, a shiftless dimwit played by Allen Jenkins. A regular character player in both comedies and serious crime films, Jenkins was a sort of all-purpose dolt in the Warners stock company. His relationship with Blondell in this story is clearly not a passionate love affair. His main interest in her seems to be her icebox; and for her part, she bridles at the suggestion of hitting him up for the money: "I've been trying to comb that mug out of my hair for months!"

Nevertheless, Jenkins has underworld connections that can provide the necessary funds to finance—as he thinks—Blondell's trip to Kansas to procure a gallstone operation for her mother. His tough boss (Ralph Ince) loans him the money, leaving no doubt as to Jenkins' fate if the loan is not repaid promptly. Within minutes Jenkins loses it all at the roulette wheel, but a fast-talking insurance salesman (Hobart Cavanaugh) inveigles him into a scheme that will replace the money with—as he believes—no risk to himself. Jenkins has thus been duped three times in the space of less than one reel, and is in far greater jeopardy than he imagines. But long before the truth can dawn on him, Blondell and Farrell are in Havana, ready to seek their fortunes.

It's significant that, having discarded so many story elements from the two earlier films, the filmmakers chose to retain *The Life of the Party*'s setting of Havana for the ladies' depredations. With the repeal of Prohibition in progress in 1933,[23] the lure of forbidden alcoholic fruit was becoming a lesser factor in bringing American tourists to Cuba; but the fascination with Cuba's exotic culture remained. The title of the new Warners film, *Havana Widows*, was assigned even before the script was written, and Jack Warner speculated that the picture would incorporate such scenes as "the main hotel in Havana, the race track, and all the atmosphere of Havana."[24] At least one major musical production number was also planned. In the end the film was scaled down considerably from these ambitious original plans,[25] but the finished version does establish a stronger ambiance than its predecessor, if only musically. North Americans' growing interest in Latin American cultures during the 1930s was driven largely by Cuban music, and the hotel scenes in *Havana Widows* are enhanced by atmospheric musical scoring. Although there is no overt production number per se, one dialogue scene is set in a nightclub and features evocative music and cutaways to a troupe of dancers.

Having arrived in the Cuban capital, Blondell and Farrell set out to locate the breach-of-promise lawyer who has been recommended to them. It doesn't take long. "Duffy" turns out to be Frank McHugh, another regular in the Warners stock company, who is staying just down the hall in the same hotel. McHugh was a versatile player who could play a range of characters as needed, from a tough newspaper editor in *Mystery of the Wax Museum* to a helpless, whining dance director in *Footlight Parade*. Here he's an alcoholic lawyer, not simply drunk but so smashed that he can barely stagger from his own room to Blondell's and Farrell's room, which he does

Footloose widows meet the Great Depression: Joan Blondell and Glenda Farrell in the seedy burlesque-house dressing room in *Havana Widows*. © Warner Bros. Courtesy George Eastman Museum.

on frequent occasions—not through any interest in them but because he has discovered that *their* doorknob makes a perfect bottle opener.

Eventually the ladies do manage to connect with McHugh, explain their mission, and agree on a strategy. The victim targeted for their breach-of-promise scheme is yet another Warners contractee: Guy Kibbee, essaying his usual specialty as a clueless, bumbling older man, ripe for fleecing. *Havana Widows* does not repeat the mistaken-identity device of the two earlier films. Instead of pursuing one man, whom they think is rich, while simultaneously falling for another man with the same name, the ladies set out to entrap the perpetually befuddled Kibbee while Blondell simultaneously falls for his son (played by Lyle Talbot), also staying at the hotel.

Havana Widows started shooting in August 1933 with George Barnes as the cameraman. This was significant because, earlier in the year, Barnes had married Joan Blondell.[26] Whatever effect this private relationship may have had on their working relationship, producer Hal

Wallis was concerned that it made for a harmful conflict of interest. "The photography on this picture is too soft," Wallis complained of the first rushes. "You have a backstage atmosphere with a burlesque show, and it is so beautiful and so highly highlighted and so glossy that all of the comedy of the scene is lost. . . . We are going to have to forget our sentiment in letting Barnes photograph Blondell's picture and get down to business . . . I am not going to horse around and make bad pictures to please a cameraman."[27] Barnes did remain on the picture, and Joan Blondell does receive the undeniable benefit of lush camerawork throughout the rest of the film—as well as several of her subsequent pictures which were *also* photographed by Barnes.

Produced in August–September 1933, *Havana Widows* qualifies as a "pre-Code" film—a term which is widely misunderstood by latter-day fans of classic films. To begin with, it's a misnomer. The Production Code actually had been written and adopted in 1930, and was in existence throughout the years that we think of as the "pre-Code" period. The change that took place in 1934 was the establishment of the Production Code Administration, the body that *enforced* the Code.[28] The intervening years did produce a wealth of films with a gritty, uncompromising view of life in the Depression years, but they were not simply a Wild West in which filmmakers freely packed their pictures with salacious content. The Hays Office still demanded the right to review screenplays before production started, *and* finished films when production was complete, and to dictate changes at both junctures. The studios could choose to ignore those dictates—but if they did, they faced a battery of state and local censor boards who would not hesitate to mutilate any offending films before they reached theater screens.

Havana Widows was no exception. Warners dutifully submitted the screenplay to the Hays Office in advance of production. Just before shooting started they received a reply from the office's James Wingate, who detailed a three-page list of passages in the script—most of them quite harmless by today's standards—which might be considered "objectionable" and should be revised or omitted. (Wallis passed along the list to supervisor Robert Lord with a note: "Please read the attached censor notes from Wingate on *Havana Widows* and, after you walk around the lot to cool off, come in and see me about it."[29]) The finished versions of those scenes represent an uneasy compromise: some of the passages are omitted, some are slightly revised, some remain substantially as written. One of Wingate's concerns was the scene in which Farrell and Blondell coax the needed money out of Allen Jenkins by manufacturing their story about Blondell's mother's gallstone operation. Farrell's dialogue was written with intentional vagueness so that Jenkins, at first, panicked at the suggestion that Blondell might need an abortion. This innuendo was not lost on Wingate, who recommended that the passage be cut from the script altogether. The dialogue remains in the finished film, modified only in the slightest degree.

Having found their way to Havana and set their sights on a victim, Blondell and Farrell get down to business. As we've noted, their scheme is nothing like the one we've seen in the two earlier films, but they're subject to just as many mishaps as the other female con artists—if anything, *more* than their share of mishaps. Their objective seems simple enough: maneuver Guy Kibbee into a compromising position with Blondell, surprise him *in flagrante delicto*, and snap some incriminating photos that can be used to launch a breach-of-promise suit. But this proves easier said than done, since McHugh can never stay sober long enough to follow through, Blondell seems unable to concentrate on anything other than Lyle Talbot, and, most problematic, Kibbee seems remarkably immune to seduction. Indeed, cowed by the presence of his wife—Ruth Donnelly, also staying at the hotel—Kibbee recoils in terror at the mere sight of Joan Blondell.

Soon enough, another complication: like Douglas Gerrard and Charles Judels before him, Allen Jenkins shows up at the hotel. Of course he's less than pleased to find that his generous loan has propelled Blondell straight into Talbot's arms. (One of the best lines in the film is Blondell's sheepish, gum-chewing quasi-apology to Jenkins: "I never lied to you, did I, Herman? Much?") Far more than this, however, Jenkins is frantic to recover the money and return it to Ralph Ince in time to save his own skin. On cue, Ince himself *also* shows up at the hotel, looking for Jenkins, and it's Jenkins' turn to flee in panic.

All these threads come together and build to a head in the film's closing reels. McHugh and the ladies mount one final, spectacularly inept, attempt to entrap Kibbee by having him kidnapped and held prisoner, in his underwear, in a locked room. A riot breaks out in the street outside, and in the excitement McHugh manages to get himself knocked out cold. Meanwhile Ince spots his quarry and pursues the terrified Jenkins through the streets and surrounding countryside. This chaotic climax is ultimately resolved happily for all, not because of the ladies' machinations, but in spite of them. Ince, it turns out, has no murderous intent toward Jenkins, but merely wants to bring him back to New York because he has decided (not very convincingly) that Jenkins' mere presence brings him good luck. Kibbee, Blondell, and Farrell, it turns out, have nothing to fear from Ruth Donnelly; on the contrary, she has been seeking a divorce and is grateful to the ladies for providing helpful evidence. Blondell, freed from the necessity of pursuing a breach-of-promise suit, happily marries Talbot, while Farrell in turn marries Jenkins for some reason. And the whole lot of them, hauled before a Cuban court, avoid the prospect of mass incarceration; instead the judge, eager to be rid of these unruly Americans, deports them *en masse* back to the States.

Havana Widows was completed and released in November 1933 to mixed reviews, and went on to modest success at the box office. In the space of less than a decade, Warner Bros. had produced three different motion pictures based loosely (very loosely) on the same story. All three films were wholly dissimilar from one another, and none of them particularly resembled the Beatrice Burton story that was, technically, their source, but each one was precisely attuned to *its moment*. The differences had been driven by a canny sensitivity to changing conditions in the industry, some of those changes instigated by the studio itself, and to evolving audience tastes. Of course those conditions and tastes continued to evolve, and in fact this particular chain of adaptation didn't exactly end with *Havana Widows*. Recognizing Joan Blondell and Glenda Farrell as a comedy team with possibilities, the studio continued to co-star them in a further series of comedies in 1934–35. None of the new pictures were sequels, with continuing stories or characters. But all were linked in spirit by their two leads: smart, funny, spirited gals, willing to play by the rules, but not above manipulating any egotistical, gullible males who got in their way—sisters under the skin to Louise Fazenda and Jacqueline Logan in 1926, and all part of the constantly shifting face of Warner Bros. comedy during its liveliest years.

Notes

1. Louise Fazenda obituary, *Variety*, 25 April 1962.
2. And with still greater frequency after 1927, when she married Warners producer Hal Wallis.
3. An important turning point occurred for Warner Bros. in 1923, when the studio became fully incorporated and obtained a $500,000 bank loan. Half the money was used to upgrade the Warners Sunset lot; the other half was invested in the purchase of three David Belasco stage properties, to be adapted for the screen. (See Schatz, *The Genius of the System*, p. 60; and "Belasco Identified with Industry," *Motion Picture News*, 27 January 1923, p. 436.) The first of the Belasco films to be produced was Avery Hopwood's *The Gold Diggers*, which had been a hit on Broadway in 1919. The film version was released in the autumn of 1923 to favorable reviews and business ("Even the prudes will like the way the Warners have done this picture," said *Variety* [13 September 1923, p. 28], "and the Warners have done it well"). The studio went on to remake the picture twice; one of the remakes, *Gold Diggers of 1933*, would remain an all-time Warners classic.
4. E.J. Meagher, reader's report, 3 September 1925 (*Footloose Widows* story file 1889B, Warner Bros. Archives, School of Cinematic Arts, University of Southern California, hereinafter identified as "WBA").
5. "Gold digger" was already a popular generic term in 1920s culture, even apart from the play and the Warners film. In the finished version of *Footloose Widows*, Louise Fazenda and Jacqueline Logan are both explicitly referred to as "gold-diggers" in one dialogue title.
6. Like many another Hollywood-produced film that tells a New York story, *Footloose Widows* establishes its setting with an opening montage of New York stock shots. This particular montage is remarkable in its extensive length and in its generous view of contemporary stage and film attractions on Broadway. The legitimate stage is represented here by *The Student Prince* at Jolson's 59th Street Theatre, *Sunny* (which would be filmed four years later by Warners/First National) at the New Amsterdam, and the current edition of the *Vanities* at the Earl Carroll Theatre; while the movie attractions include *The Lost World* at the Astor, *Sackcloth and Scarlet* at Loew's, *The Black Pirate* at the Selwyn, *Beverly of Graustark* at the Capitol, and, of course, the Rin Tin Tin picture *The Night Cry* at the Warner. At least one reviewer commented on all the "free advertising" in this opening sequence (*Footloose Widows* review, *Variety* ["Fred"], 23 June 1926, p. 14).
7. In 2002, when I was first researching this film for the Giornate, David Robinson suggested that this scene had been inserted as a favor to Swain, who had costarred with Fazenda a decade earlier in some of her first Keystone appearances. I'm inclined to agree.
8. See note 3.
9. In 1926, of course, Mack Sennett's independent studio was still alive and well and releasing a string of successful comedies to theaters.
10. Barrios, *A Song in the Dark*, p. 192.

11. The oddity in this group was *She Couldn't Say No*, which was *not* filmed in Technicolor and in which Lightner did essay some serious torch songs. Reaction to this side of her persona was mixed at best, and the studio never repeated this experiment. See Barrios, *A Song in the Dark*, p. 208.
12. Zanuck was such a prolific writer that he wrote scripts for the studio under four different names, including his own. (See Schatz, *The Genius of the System*, p. 62.) He had written *Footloose Widows* in 1926 as Darryl F. Zanuck, but in 1930 Warners contracted with him to write the new sound film under one of his pseudonyms, Mark Canfield. When the finished film was shown in theaters, it was another Zanuck alias, Melville Crossman, that appeared in the screen credits.
13. The film actually begins with another montage of the bright lights of Broadway, similar to the opening of *Footloose Widows*. Since we've already observed the earlier sequence in detail, we might note that this one follows the 1926 precedent: a generous selection of electric signs advertising contemporary stage and screen attractions playing on Broadway. This time there's a heavier proportion of Warner Bros. titles: *Song of the Flame*, *Courage*, and *Fifty Million Frenchmen*.
14. "Warner Production at Season's Peak," *Film Daily*, 9 June 1930, p. 5.
15. See Layton and Pierce, *The Dawn of Technicolor*, pp. 116 and 124.
16. Delroy's successful fashion-show turn in widow's weeds is followed by a dialogue exchange with Lightner about widows' irresistible appeal to men: "To a man, a widow is like finding another drink in the bottle when he thought it was empty." After this and other less-than-subtle observations, the audience can scarcely miss the point.
17. See Kaufman, *Pinocchio*, p. 92.
18. *The Life of the Party* dialogue continuity, 28 August 1930 (WBA).
19. See Okrent, *Last Call*, pp. 217–18.
20. See Schatz, *The Genius of the System*, pp. 152–55.
21. Since we've observed the opening New York montages in the two earlier films, it's appropriate to point out the corresponding scene in this one. In context—after seeing the openings of *Footloose Widows* and *Life of the Party*, with their atmosphere of immersion in the dazzling glamor of Broadway—the opening of *Havana Widows* seems almost like an in-joke: two quick overhead shots of city lights, followed immediately by the exterior of the seedy burlesque house, with its marquee promising "Iwanna Shakitoff, Direct from Russia With Her Forty Beautiful Hip Hip Hooray Girls." Although this shabby showplace is far removed from the opulent world of *42nd Street*, the chorus line onstage is dancing to "Pretty Lady," the instrumental tune that Harry Warren had composed for the show-within-the-film in *42nd Street*.
22. Memo, Jack L. Warner to Hal Wallis, 25 May 1933, subject: HAVANA WIDOWS (*Havana Widows* production file 1955B, WBA).
23. Repeal was actually a gradual process that occurred in stages during 1933. Shortly after Franklin D. Roosevelt took office in March, Congress convened and loosened the strictures on beer. The full repeal of the 18th Amendment was a more complicated undertaking and was not completed until December, after *Havana Widows* had been released.

24. Memo, Warner to Wallis, 25 May 1933, subject: HAVANA WIDOWS (*Havana Widows* production file 1955B, WBA).
25. Warners publicity later claimed that the studio had planned to send a second unit to Havana to shoot some authentic scenery, but when the revolutionary riots broke out in Cuba in August 1933, concurrently with the start of production, "the producers . . . conferred for a few minutes and decided to build sets right in Burbank" ("Revolutions Are Easy for Hollywood to Cope With," undated Warner Bros. press release, *Havana Widows* production file 681B, WBA).
26. "Joan Blondell Wed," *New York Times*, 5 January 1933, 19:7.
27. Memo, Wallis to William Koenig, 10 August 1933, subject: HAVANA WIDOWS (*Havana Widows* production file 1955B, WBA).
28. See Leff and Simmons, *The Dame in the Kimono*, pp. 9–17 and 54–56.
29. Memo, Wallis to Lord, 8 August 1933, subject: HAVANA WIDOWS (*Havana Widows* production file 1955B, WBA).

Footloose Widows

Warner Bros., 19 June 1926
Copyright (as *Footloose Windows* [sic]) 18 June 1926 by Warner Bros. Pictures, Inc. (LP22825)
7 reels (7163 ft)

Director: Roy Del Ruth
Scenario: Darryl F. Zanuck, based on *Footloose* by Beatrice Burton
Titles: Robert Hopkins
Art titles: Victor Vance
Camera: David Abel
        assistant: Charles Van Enger
Film editor: H.P. Bretherton
Assistant director: William McGann
CAST: Louise Fazenda (Flo)
        Jacqueline Logan (Marion)
        Jason Robards (Jerry)
        Arthur Hoyt (Henry)
        Neely Edwards (McGill)
        Mack Swain (Marion's [fictional] late husband)
        John Miljan (J.A. Smith)
        Henry Barrows (hotel manager)

The Life of the Party

Warner Bros., 25 October 1930
Copyright 2 October 1930 by Warner Bros. Pictures, Inc. (LP1602)
8 reels (7152 ft)

Director: Roy Del Ruth
Scenario: Arthur Caesar, based on a story by Melville Crossman [Zanuck]
Camera: Dev Jennings
Film editor: William Holmes
CAST: Winnie Lightner (Flo)
Irene Delroy (Dot)
Jack Whiting (A.J. Smith)
Charles Butterworth (Col. Joy)
Charles Judels (M. Le Maire)
Arthur Edmund Carewe (fake count)
John Davidson (bogus Mr. Smith)
Arthur Hoyt (secretary)

Havana Widows

First National, 18 November 1933
Copyright 18 November 1933 by First National Pictures, Inc. (LP4252)
7 reels

Director: Ray Enright
Screenplay: Earl Baldwin
Camera: George Barnes
Film editor: Clarence Koster
CAST: Joan Blondell (Mae Knight)
Glenda Farrell (Sadie Appleby)
Guy Kibbee (Deacon Jones)
Allen Jenkins (Herman Brody)
Lyle Talbot (Bob Jones)
Frank McHugh (Duffy)
Ruth Donnelly (Mrs. Jones)
Hobart Cavanaugh (Mr. Otis)
Ralph Ince (Butch O'Neill)
Maude Eburne (Mrs. Ryan)
George Cooper (Mullins)
Charles Wilson (Timberg)
Garry Owen (wheelman)

Uncredited: Renee Whitney (chorine), Noel Francis (Gladys Gable), Dewey Robinson, John Kelly (kidnappers)

Volume 2 Bibliography

Articles

Erik Barnouw, "The Sintzenich Diaries," *Quarterly Journal of the Library of Congress*, Summer/Fall 1980

DeWitt Bodeen, "Blanche Sweet" [career article], *Films in Review*, November 1965, pp. 549–570

William K. Everson, "Random Thoughts on the 'Best Picture' vs. the 'Best Director'," *Films in Review*, December 1986, pp. 594–98

Luther Hathcock, "Whatever Happened to Cowboy Star Jack Luden?", *Classic Images*, vol. 145 (July 1987), pp. 13–16

Gregory Mank, "Marian Marsh Recalls Filming Svengali with Barrymore," *Films in Review*, December 1985, pp. 578–82

Roi A. Uselton, "The Wampas Baby Stars," *Films in Review*, February 1970, pp. 73–97

Books

Richard Barrios, *A Song in the Dark: The Birth of the Musical Film* (New York and Oxford: Oxford, 1995)

Kevin Brownlow, *The Parade's Gone By . . .* (New York: Knopf, 1968)

_____, *The War, the West, and the Wilderness* (New York: Knopf, 1979)

Craig W. Campbell, *Reel America and World War I* (Jefferson NC and London: McFarland, 1985)

Paolo Cherchi Usai, Lorenzo Codelli (eds.), *L'eredità DeMille/The DeMille Legacy* (Pordenone: Le Giornate del Cinema Muto/Edizioni Biblioteca dell'Immagine, 1991)

William K. Everson, *The Art of W.C. Fields* (Indianapolis, Kansas City, New York: Bobbs-Merrill, 1967)

_____, *American Silent Film* (New York: Oxford, 1978)

Kathleen Karr (ed.), *The American Film Heritage: Impressions from the American Film Institute Archives* (Washington: Acropolis, 1972)

J.B. Kaufman, *Pinocchio: The Making of the Disney Epic* (San Francisco: Walt Disney Family Foundation Press, 2015)

Richard Koszarski, *The Astoria Studio and Its Fabulous Films* (New York: Dover, 1983)

_____, *Hollywood on the Hudson: Film and Television in New York from Griffith to Sarnoff* (New Brunswick NJ and London: Rutgers, 2008)

Jesse L. Lasky (with Don Weldon), *I Blow My Own Horn* (Garden City NY: Doubleday, 1957)

James Layton and David Pierce, *The Dawn of Technicolor, 1915–1935* (Rochester NY: George Eastman House, 2015)

Leonard J. Leff and Jerold L. Simmons, *The Dame in the Kimono: Hollywood, Censorship, and the Production Code* (second edition) (Lexington: University Press of Kentucky, 2001)

Leonard Maltin, *The Great Movie Shorts: Those Wonderful One- and Two-Reelers of the Thirties and Forties* (New York: Bonanza, 1972)

Daniel Okrent, *Last Call: The Rise and Fall of Prohibition* (New York, London, Toronto, Sydney: Scribner, 2010)

Ginger Rogers, *Ginger: My Story* (New York: HarperCollins, 1991)

Thomas Schatz, *The Genius of the System: Hollywood Filmmaking in the Studio Era* (New York: Pantheon, 1988)

INDEX

References in the endnotes are denoted here by page number and note number.
Page numbers in *italics* refer to illustrations.

A

Accent on Youth (stage, 1935)	38–39
Across the Pacific (1942)	41
"Adams, K." *see* Elizabeth Hardwick	
Akeley cameras	69, 80, 81
Alderson, Erville	60, 63, 64, 66, 67, 68, 70, 73, 76, 77, 79, 83
Allerton Hotel for Men (NY)	23
Allerton Hotel for Women (NY)	23
Allworth, Frank	76, 80, 81, 83, 84
Alvine, Glenn	32
America (1924)	76
American Film Institute	39
Anders, Glenn	62, 65, 66, 67
Anderson, E.H.	11
Anderson, John Murray	32
Andrews, Robert	21, 36, *34*
Applegate, Roy	64, 70
Astoria studio (Paramount)	27, 28, 44 (n. 19), 58, 83, 88 (n. 5), 89 (n. 13)
Atlantic City Beauty Pageant	20
Auditorium Hotel (Chicago)	74
Auer, Florence	82, 84
Awful Truth, The (1937)	98

B

Baldwin, Earl	117
Balmer, Edwin	59, 67, 74, 75, 76, 79
Barnes, George	120–21
Barrios, Richard	111

Barry, Wesley	8
Barrymore, John	40
Barrymore, Lionel	102 (n. 2)
Bayside (NY)	70
Beasts of Berlin (1939)	41
Beau Geste (1926)	30
Beery, Wallace	8, *9*
Bell, Monta	83, 85
Ben-Hur (1925)	26, 44 (n. 22)
Benchley, Robert	97, 98
Berkeley, Busby	40
Betteridge, May	20
Beverly of Graustark (1926)	124 (n. 6)
Birth of a Nation, The (1915)	12
Black Pirate, The (1926)	124 (n. 6)
Blackstone Hotel (Chicago)	74
Blackton, Greg	19, 23, 25, 27, 28, 32, 33–35, 38, *24, 34*
Blondell, Joan	118–123, *120*
Bodeen, DeWitt	8
Boston Post, The	22
Bourne, Whitney	97–100
Bow, Clara	29
Bradbury, James Sr.	32
Bravermann, Barnet	56, 58–84
Brenon, Herbert	83
Broad Minded (1931)	38
Broadway Butterfly, A (1925)	106
Broadway Strand Theater (Detroit)	11, 12
Brockmeyer, T.A.	84
Brokaw, Charles	21, 30, 41, *34*
Brown, Joe E.	38, 111
Brownlow, Kevin	5, 39
Buchanan, Claud	22, 33, 35, 36
Burton, Beatrice	106, 107, 109, 117, 123
Bush, W. Stephen	53
Butterworth, Charles	115

C

CNC Archives (France)	102 (n. 2)
Cabijos, Marcel	25

Canadian, The (1926)	39
Canfield, Mark *see* Darryl F. Zanuck	
Cannon, Regina	31
Cantor, Eddie	40
Cappy Ricks (1921)	73
Carewe, Edwin	41
Carroll, Nancy	37
Case, Miss	69, 80, 81, 82
Cavanaugh, Hobart	119
Chambers, Marie	72, 85
Chaplin, Charlie	109
Chase, Charley	38
Chicago	33, 34, 72–76
Chicago Evening Post	76
Christy, Howard Chandler	20
Cineteca del Friuli, La	4
Clarendon, Hal	25
Clark, C.E.	34
Clive, Henry	40
Close Harmony (1929)	37
Cockeyed Cavaliers (1934)	38
Coen, Franklin	98
Cohill, William	19
Committee on Public Information	9
Cook County Jail	76, 84
Cooper, Merian C.	93, 94, 102 (n. 1)
Corbett, James	70
Cosmopolitan magazine	59
Courage (1930)	125 (n. 13)
Cowl, Jane	21, 41
"Creel Committee" *see* Committee on Public Information	
Crews, Laura Hope	97
Crossman, Melville *see* Darryl F. Zanuck	
Crute, Sally	84
Currie, George	25
Curtiss Aeroplane	80, 82

D

Dalton, Frank E.	25
Daniels, Bebe	61, 62, 63, 71

Davidson, Dore	77
Davidson, John	115, 116
del Río, Dolores	41
Del Ruth, Roy	109, 111–12, 113, 115, 116, 117
DeMille, Cecil B.	54 (n. 7)
De Titta, Arthur	79–80
Delroy, Irene	112–17, 118, 125 (n. 16), *113*
Dempster, Carol	60–85, 74
Depths, The (stage, 1925)	21
Dewey, Arthur	76, 78
Diem, Frank	60, 62, 63, 64, 67
Dillon, Wilbur	22–23
Disney, Walt	114
Dix, Richard	29, 32, 83, 102 (n. 2)
Dodd, Mead and Co.	59
Doherty, Ethel	36
Donnelly, Dorothy	59
Donnelly, Ruth	122
Double Harness (1933)	102 (n. 2)
Douglastown (NY)	69, 82, 84
Drew, Roland	40–41, 42
Dunn, James	97–100
Dunn, Josephine	20, 27, 35, 36, 38–39, 42, *34*
Dunne, Irene	102 (n. 2)
Dupe, The (1916)	54 (n. 7)

E

Earl Carroll's Vanities	124 (n. 6)
Eason, Lorraine	22–23, 43 (n. 15)
Easy Living (1937)	98
Edwards, Neely	110, 115
Emerson, John	18
Enright, Ray	117
Evangeline (1929)	41
Everson, William K.	88 (n. 1), 95
Everton, Paul	79, 80, 82, 83, 84
Excella magazine	20
Excess Baggage (1938)	38
Exhibitors Trade Review	36, 85

F

Famous Players-Lasky	18, 22, 57, 59, 60, 67, 71, 72, 77, 86–87
Fascinating Youth (1926)	17, 27–32, 47
Fascinating Youth tour	32–35
Farrell, Glenda	118–123, *120*
Fazenda, Louise	105–10, 111, 112, 115, 116, 118, 123, 124 (n. 5 and 7), *108*
Fields, W.C.	25–26, 36, 40, 43–44 (n. 19), 57–71, 73, 77–87, *61*
Fifty Million Frenchmen (1931)	125 (n. 13)
First National Pictures	110
Fischbeck, Harry	60, 65, 66, 67, 71, 77, 78, 79, 85
Flagg, James Montgomery	20
Flash Gordon Conquers the Universe (1940)	41
Florida	109–10, 114
Flushing (NY)	68, 70, 79
Follow Thru (1930)	37
Fontanne, Lynn	62
Footlight Parade (1933)	119
"Footloose" (serialized story, 1925)	106, 107
Footloose Widows (1926)	106–10, 124 (n. 6)
Ford, Harrison	72, 73, 75, 77, 78, 83, 84
Ford, John	94
Forman, Tom	53
42nd Street (1933)	94, 117, 118, 125 (n. 21)
Foster, Norman	94–100, 102 (n. 3), *96, 99*
Foxe, Earle	52–53
Francis, Noel	118
Frohman, Daniel	18

G

Garson, Harry	5–6, 8, 10–12
"Gateway to Hollywood" (radio, 1939)	42
George White's Scandals (stage, 1925)	78
Gerrard, Douglas	108, 109–10, 114, 120, 122, *108*
Get Your Man (1927)	38
Gilbert, Paul	76
Gilson, Charles	81
Giornate del Cinema Muto, Le	*10*
Girl of Today (unfinished, 1932)	86
Gish, Dorothy	21

Gish, Lillian	39
Glorious Youth see *Fascinating Youth*	
Gold Diggers, The (1923)	106, 107, 124 (n. 3)
Gold Diggers of Broadway (1929)	111
Gold Diggers of 1933 (1933)	94, 118, 124 (n. 3)
Gold Rush, The (1925)	109
Goldwyn Pictures	61
Goodbye, Mr. Chips (1939)	26
Goss, Walter	21, 33, 36, 40–41
Grand Central Station	76
Grandona, Mme. E.	25
Gray, Iris	23, 28, 33–35, 36, 40, *29*, *34*
Great Neck (NY)	70, 71
Greenwich (CT)	68, 70
Grey, Albert	85
Griffith, D.W.	18, 36, 44 (n. 19), 56, 57–86, *74*
Griffithiana	4, 48, 56
Guardsman, The (stage, 1925)	62

H

Hall, Mordaunt	77
Hammond, Charles	65
Hampton, Jesse D.	12
Harding, Ann	102 (n. 2)
Hardwick, Elizabeth	51
Harper & Brothers	6
Harris, Marian Ivy	20, 27, 35, 36, 40, *29*, *34*
Hartley, Irving	21, *34*
Hathcock, Luther	39
Hatton, Raymond	53
Havana	114, 119, 126 (n. 25)
Havana Widows (1933)	117–123, 125 (n. 21), *120*
Hays Office	121
Heads Up (1930)	37
Hearst's International magazine	59
Hergesheimer, Joseph	18
Herzog, Dorothy	31
Hicksville (NY)	68
Hippodrome	85
Hips, Hips, Hooray (1934)	38

Hold Everything (1930)	111
Hopwood, Avery	107, 124 (n. 3)
Horse Feathers (1932)	38
Horton, Margaret Weaver	51
Hot-Cha! (stage, 1932)	37
Howard, Sidney	41, 62
Hoyt, Arthur	116
Hudson, Rochelle	87
Hughes, Rupert	6–7
Hunt, J. Roy	60, 61, 62, 63, 64, 65, 85
Huntington (NY)	69
Hushed Hour, The (1919)	6, 12

I

I Cover the War (1937)	41
Ince, Ralph	119, 122
Islip (NY)	69
Isn't Life Wonderful (1924)	56, 60
It Happened One Night (1934)	98
It's a Gift (1934)	87
It's Love I'm After (1937)	98

J

Jackson Heights (NY)	71, 79
Jazz Singer, The (1927)	110, 111
Jenkins, Allen	118–19, 121–23
Jim (lion)	61
Jolson, Al	38
Jordan, Dorothy	102 (n. 1)
Judels, Charles	112, 114, 116, 122, *113*

K

Kane, Eddie	112
Kane, Helen	37
Kansas University	19, 25, 37
Keaton, Buster	38
Kelly, Patsy	38
Kennedy, Tom	97–98
Kenvin, Ethelda (Thelda)	20, 35, *34*
Keystone Film Company	106, 109, 110, 124 (n. 7)

Kibbee, Guy	120, 122
King on Main Street, The (1925)	85
Kirkwood, James	72, 73, 75, 76, 77, 78, 79, 81, 82, 83
Klaw Theatre	62
Koszarski, Richard	16, 56
Krauth, Harriet *see* Jeanne Morgan	
Krauth, Violet *see* Marian Marsh	

L

La Cava, Gregory	25–26
La Sylphe, Mlle.	25
Laidley, Alice	77
Lake Michigan	76
Lake Placid (NY)	28–29
Lamb, Arthur	*13*
Land of Promise, The (stage, 1913)	39
Landers, Lew	100
Langdon, Harry	38
Lasky, Blanche	54 (n. 7)
Lasky, Jesse L.	18, 25, 30, 41–42
Laurel and Hardy	38
Leu, Berniece see Iris Gray	
Libeled Lady (1936)	98
Library of Congress	48, 58
Life of the Party, The (1930)	111–17, 125 (n. 13), *113*
Lightner, Winnie	111–17, 118, 125 (n. 11), *113*
Lindsay, Laverne (Sharon Lynn)	22–23, 43 (n. 15)
Living on Love (1937)	97–101, 102 (n. 2)
Logan, Jacqueline	107–10, 112, 114, 118, 123, 124 (n. 5), *108*
Long, Louise	36
Long Island City	68
Long Island Motor Parkway	69
Long Island Speedway	69
Loomis (stunt driver)	69
Lord, Robert	121
Lost Patrol, The (1934)	94
Lost World, The (1925)	124 (n. 6)
Love, Dorothea	78
Low, Joe	79–80, 85
Lubitsch, Ernst	95

Lucy (elephant)	62
Luden, Jack	21–22, 25, 33, 36, 39, 42
Lunt, Alfred	62, 64, 65, 66, 68, 70
Lynch, Frank	40
Lytton, Morgia	25

M

MacMahon, Aline	118
McHugh, Frank	119–20, 122
Man to Remember, A (1938)	102 (n. 2)
Manhandled (1924)	73
Marsh, Marian	40, 42
Marx Brothers	38
Matz, Madeline	56
Maugham, Somerset	39
Meeker, Mary	75
Meighan, Thomas	18, 83
Menjou, Adolphe	29, 83
Metro-Goldwyn-Mayer	38
Miles Projection Rooms	64, 68, 73
Miljan, John	109
Millay, Dennis	93–94, 101, 102 (n. 2)
Miller, Gilbert	18
Miller, William	81, 88–89 (n. 13)
Miller Theater (Wichita KS)	34–35
Million Dollar Legs (1932)	87
Monkey Business (1931)	38
Morgan, Byron	27
Morgan, Jeanne	22, 30, 33, 36, 40, *29*
Morgan, Marilyn see Marian Marsh	
Motion Picture magazine	31–32
Motion Picture Classic magazine	32
Moving Picture World, The	12, 53
Museum of Modern Art	58
My Best Girl (1927)	37
My Man Godfrey (1936)	98
Mystery of the Wax Museum (1933)	119

N

Neilan, Marshall	5, 8, 11, 12
New Amsterdam Theatre	60
New York Dramatic Mirror, The	49
New York Graphic, The	31
New York Herald Tribune, The	21
New York Mirror, The	31
New York Times, The	11, 18, 54 (n. 4), 77, 102 (n. 2)
New York World, The	21
Night at the Opera, A (1935)	26
Night Cry, The (1926)	124 (n. 6)
Nothing Sacred (1937)	98
Nourse, Dorothy	22, 33, 36, *29, 34*

O

Office Blues (1930)	94
Old Ironsides (1926)	30
One Hour With You (1932)	38
One Man's Journey (1933)	102 (n. 1 and 2)

P

Palace Theater (Superior WI)	12
Palma, Mona	20, 23, 33, 36, 39, 42
Pangborn, Franklin	98
Parade's Gone By ..., The (Brownlow)	44 (n. 22)
Paramount on Parade (1930)	37
Paramount Pictures School	16–47, 88 (n. 10)
Paramount Stock Company School	17–18
Patchogue (NY)	71
Paths of Glory (stage, 1935)	41
Paton, Charles	41
Peck, Catherine	50
Peck, Clara	50, 51, 52–53
Peck, John E.	50, 51
Peck, Percy	50, 51, 53
Pelswick, Rose	27
Pennsylvania Station (NY)	114
Peters, George	81
Phillips, Nancy	36
Pitts, ZaSu	38

Photoplay magazine	7, 18
Photo-Play Journal	10
Pickford, Mary	8, 37
Pilgrim, The (1923)	109
Pinocchio (1940)	114
Poppy (stage, 1923)	58, 59, 60
Poppy (1936)	87
Potters, The (1927)	40
Powell, William	102 (n. 2)
Professional Sweetheart (1933)	94, 102 (n. 3)
Prohibition	114, 119, 125 (n. 23)
Public Opinion (1916)	48–55, *52*

R

RKO Radio Pictures	93–94
Rafter Romance (1933)	92–101, 102 (n. 1 and 2), *96, 99*
Ramona (1928)	41
Raphaelson, Samson	38
Red Bank NJ	29, *29*
Red Book magazine	6
Reichert, Catherine "Kittens"	26
Reid, Wallace	27
Richards Air Field (Kansas City)	34
Ritz-Carlton Hotel (NY)	30
Rivoli Theatre (NY)	32
Roach, Hal	37, 38
Road to Rome, The (stage, 1927)	41
Robards, Jason	109, 110
Robinson, David	124 (n. 7)
Rogers, C.A.	35
Rogers, Charles "Buddy"	19, 20, 21, 23, 25, 26, 27, 30, 32–33, 35, 36, 37, 38, 39, 41, 42, 43–44 (n. 19), *34*
Rogers, Ginger	94–100, 102 (n. 1 and 3), *96, 99*
Rolled Stockings (1927)	36–37
Roosevelt, Franklin D.	117, 125 (n. 23)
Roosevelt Theatre (Chicago)	75
Roslyn (NY)	69
Rubber Heels (1927)	36, 73
Running Wild (1927)	87

S

Sackcloth and Scarlet (1925)	124 (n. 6)
Safety in Numbers (1930)	38
Sally of the Sawdust (1925)	57–75, 76, 77, 80, 82, 86, *61*
Seiter, William A.	94–100
Sennett, Mack	106, 124 (n. 9)
Shannon, Effie	60, 63, 64, 66
She Couldn't Say No (1930)	111, 125 (n. 11)
She Cried for the Moon (stage, 1935)	39
Sheiks and Shebas see *Rolled Stockings*	
Shock Punch, The (1925)	88–89 (n. 13)
Shootin' Irons (1927)	39
Shop Around the Corner, The (1940)	95
Show Girl in Hollywood (1930)	46 (n. 64)
Show of Shows, The (1929)	111
Shrewsbury River	29
Sidney, George	96–97, 100
Silvers, Louis	72
Sing Sing	53
Singing Fool, The (1928)	38
Sintzenich, Hal	56, 58–86, *74*
Slattery, Charles	71
Sleep, My Love (1948)	26
Smith, Agnes	27, 28
Smith, H.M.K.	25
Son of a Sailor (1933)	38
Song of the Flame (1930)	125 (n. 13)
Sorrows of Satan, The (1926)	36, 60, 80, 86
So's Your Old Man (1926)	26, 44 (n. 19)
Spanish influenza epidemic	8
Sparks Circus	71
Speak Easily (1932)	38
Steiner, Bill	78
Stingaree (1934)	102 (n. 2)
Stone, John	56
Strand Theatre (NY)	77
Stroheim, Erich von	97
Student Prince, The (stage, 1924)	124 (n. 6)
Sunny (stage, 1925)	124 (n. 6)
Sunny (1930)	124 (n. 6)

Sutherland, Eddie	87
Svengali (1931)	40
Swain, Mack	109, 124 (n. 7)
Swanson, Gloria	26, 28, 30, 83
Sweet, Blanche	4–14, 48–55, *9, 13, 52*
Syosset (NY)	67, 68

T

TCM (Turner Classic Movies)	93–94, 101
Talbot, Lyle	120, 122
"Tarzan" films	61
Taylor, Mrs. J. Walter	23
Technicolor	111, 113
Temple, Shirley	97
Terriss, Tom	26, 44 (n. 20)
That Royle Girl (novel) (1924–25)	59, 67
That Royle Girl (1925)	43–44 (n. 19), 57, 59, 72–86, *74*
They Knew What They Wanted (stage, 1925)	62
This Woman (1924)	106
Todd, Thelma	20–21, 27, 33, 35, 36, 37–38, 42, *34*
Toomey, John G.	25
Tover, Leo	26
Treasurer's Report, The (1929)	97
Troye, Hans	29
Tsiantis, Lee	93–94, 101, 102 (n. 2)
Turnbull, Margaret	49–50, 51, 53, 54 (n. 7)

U

United Artists	59, 71, 86
Universal Pictures	106
Unpardonable Sin, The (1919)	4–14
Uptown Theater (Chicago)	34

V

Van de Water, Virginia Terhune	25
Vandiver, Florence M.	20
Variety	12, 32, 86, 106, 124 (n. 3 and 6)
Varsity (1928)	37
Vitaphone	110, 111

W

Waite, Arthur Warren	50–54
Wallis, Hal	120–21, 124 (n. 2)
Wampas Baby Stars	38
War, the West, and the Wilderness, The (Brownlow)	5
Ward, Robert *see* Walter Goss	
Warner, Harry	117
Warner, Jack	119
Warner Bros.	104–123, 124 (n. 3)
Warren, Harry	125 (n. 21)
Warrens of Virginia, The (1924)	21
Waterman, Ida	72, 77
Watson, Bobby	77, 78
Weaver, Alice	78
Webber, George	85
Wellman, William	37
We're in the Navy Now (1926)	43 (n. 15)
Western Electric	110
Wheeler and Woolsey	38
Whitestone (NY)	71
Whiting, Jack	115, 116
Whoopee! (1930)	40
Wichita (KS) Municipal Airport	34
Wild, Wild Susan (1925)	71
Williams, Guinn "Big Boy"	97, 99
Williams, Kathlyn	61
Wilson, Lois	29
Wilson, Woodrow	9
Wind, The (1928)	39
Wingate, James	121
Wings (1927)	30, 37
Wood, Sam	26, 27
Woolf Brothers Department Store (Kansas City)	35
Wynn, Ed	36, 73

Y

Young, Tammany	62
Young Eagles (1930)	37, 39
Young Man of Manhattan (1930)	102 (n. 3)

Z

Zanuck, Darryl F.   107, 109, 111–12, 113, 115, 116, 117, 125 (n. 12)
Ziegfeld, Florenz   37, 86
Ziegfeld Follies   58, 60, 64, 75, 86
Zukor, Adolph   18, 71

GREENVIEW
PRESS

ALSO AVAILABLE FROM GREENVIEW PRESS

KAUFMAN AT THE MOVIES

Articles & Essays 1987–2021
Volume 1

J.B. KAUFMAN

Merbabies: **The Disney Film That Wasn't**
  [first published 1987]

Before Snow White
  [first published 1993]

The Transcontinental Making of *The Barn Dance*
  [first published 1997]

Tanglefoot 3.0
  [first published 1998 (first version), 2011 (second version)]

A Couple of Goofs
  [not previously published]

The Heir Apparent
  [first published 2011]

www.ingramcontent.com/pod-product-compliance
Lightning Source LLC
Chambersburg PA
CBHW051130160426
43195CB00014B/2411